mindset for success

The Powerful Partnership of
Problem-Based Learning & PLC at Work®

TERRY GOODIN

HEATHER K. DILLARD

FOREWORD BY ROBERT EAKER

Solution Tree | Press

Copyright © 2025 by Solution Tree Press

Materials appearing here are copyrighted. With one exception, all rights are reserved. Readers may reproduce only those pages marked "Reproducible." Otherwise, no part of this book may be reproduced or transmitted in any form or by any means (electronic, photocopying, recording, or otherwise) without prior written permission of the publisher.

555 North Morton Street
Bloomington, IN 47404
800.733.6786 (toll free) / 812.336.7700
FAX: 812.336.7790

email: info@SolutionTree.com
SolutionTree.com

Visit **go.SolutionTree.com/PLCbooks** to download the free reproducibles in this book.

Printed in the United States of America

Library of Congress Cataloging-in-Publication Data

Names: Goodin, Terry Lynn, author. | Dillard, Heather K., author.
Title: Mindset for success : the powerful partnership of problem-based learning and PLC at work / Terry Goodin, Heather K. Dillard.
Description: Bloomington, IN : Solution Tree Press, 2024. | Includes bibliographical references and index.
Identifiers: LCCN 2024003811 (print) | LCCN 2024003812 (ebook) | ISBN 9781958590577 (paperback) | ISBN 9781958590584 (ebook)
Subjects: LCSH: Problem-based learning. | Professional learning communities.
Classification: LCC LB1027.42 .G66 2024 (print) | LCC LB1027.42 (ebook) | DDC 371.1--dc23/eng/20240222
LC record available at https://lccn.loc.gov/2024003811
LC ebook record available at https://lccn.loc.gov/2024003812

Solution Tree
Jeffrey C. Jones, CEO
Edmund M. Ackerman, President

Solution Tree Press
President and Publisher: Douglas M. Rife
Associate Publishers: Todd Brakke and Kendra Slayton
Editorial Director: Laurel Hecker
Art Director: Rian Anderson
Copy Chief: Jessi Finn
Senior Production Editor: Suzanne Kraszewski
Proofreader: Sarah Ludwig
Cover and Text Designer: Abigail Bowen
Acquisitions Editors: Carol Collins and Hilary Goff
Assistant Acquisitions Editor: Elijah Oates
Content Development Specialist: Amy Rubenstein
Associate Editor: Sarah Ludwig
Editorial Assistant: Anne Marie Watkins

To Dora Lee Goodin: As my loving mother, you've always modeled learning for me. As a child, watching you advance your own learning, I learned never to give up. Watching you teach, or design your library, I learned to strive for excellence—to get things right. We always shared ideas. We still do, and you help me make sense of the world and reach for the future. Much love, your son.

—Terry

To Hope Key Dillard: I dedicate this book to you because if it is not good enough for you, it is not good enough for anyone's child. All my love, Mom.

—Heather

Acknowledgments

This book would not exist were it not for our mentor and friend Robert Eaker, one of the architects of the Professional Learning Communities at Work® (PLCs at Work) process. Bob first saw the link between problem-based learning (PBL) and Professional Learning Communities at Work, and he encouraged us to share our experiences related to how the two approaches naturally complement each other. He walked along with us as we wrote this book, and his constant support and guidance have contributed immeasurably to the formation of the ideas we share here. Bob, saying, "thank you" is not enough; you have our heartfelt thanks and grateful appreciation.

The ideas in this book took root in 2008 with Terry's work with a team of educators at the Tennessee Board of Regents (TBR) as they redesigned the teacher education program in the state of Tennessee. Each of the six state TBR universities was to adopt a residency model for teacher preparation. The program, called Ready2Teach, was built on the problem-based learning model as presented in this book.

We wish to thank Sidney A. McPhee, president of Middle Tennessee State University (MTSU), for his substantial support of Terry in the Tennessee teacher education redesign at the Board of Regents and in a special course he and Terry taught together in which McPhee was the instructor of record.

Special thanks to Kyle Butler and Jim Huffman for their work in the initial design of the Residency I secondary-level program at Middle Tennessee State University that began in 2008. In 2013, we began working with Nancy Caukin and Steve Bartos to build on that foundation to build and finalize this groundbreaking, problem-based learning approach to teacher education at the secondary level. Residency I was a singular blending of PBL with PLC at Work. In 2016, it received national recognition as a finalist for the Outstanding Program in Education Award given by the Association of Teacher Education.

We would like to acknowledge the many caring, competent colleagues with whom we have worked as part of Residency I since its implementation in the fall of 2013. Instructors, collaborators, and professional team members learning in community include Steve Bartos, Robin Bollman, Lando Carter, Nancy Caukin, Ann Collette, Kim Evert, Heather Green, Nadine Harris, Sharron Hofer, Ashley Hover, Julia Maddux, Brad Parton, Fonya Scott, Josh Tipton, Tom Vasser, Butch Vaughn, Sarah Warner (Sister Cecilia Anne), Beth Wright, and a host of graduate assistants. We gratefully acknowledge the support of Jim Huffman, chair of the Department of Educational Leadership, and

Lana Seivers, dean of the College of Education. Though many of these fine people have moved on to other challenges, they have left a lasting impression on what remains a vital and vibrant undertaking. We also appreciate the continued support of current administrators Donald Snead, chair of the Department of Educational Leadership, and Neporcha Cone, dean of the College of Education.

The team at Solution Tree Press has been professional, collegial, and collaborative. It's a joy to work with such fine people. They truly do stand out as leaders in the field, and they do so by treating others so well. We'd like to thank Jeff Jones and Douglas Rife, who, with Bob Eaker, recognized the important link between PBL and PLC at Work, and their support is much appreciated. We thank the editorial and design team at Solution Tree for improving our work through their consummate skills, and we thank them sincerely.

From Terry: I owe much to my dissertation committee chair, Wil Clouse, my first mentor at Vanderbilt University. When I joined him as his graduate assistant in 1997, Wil spread the buffet of educational choices before me and encouraged me to explore them and find my own way. He included me in every phase of his work, which revealed to me the connections between PBL, preK–12 education, higher education, and education in the corporate world. He gave me the liberty to co-develop the Entrepreneurs in Action curriculum with him, which I and others used as the vehicle for our doctoral dissertations. Wil took me to countless conferences, which gave me valuable experience, broadened my outlook, and influenced my development as a PBL practitioner and researcher. To this day, Wil remains a true friend and enthusiastic supporter.

I want to thank my colleague and coauthor, Heather Dillard, for her contribution to this book. Since 2013, we have shared the ups and downs of program design, course design, lesson planning, teaching, and innovation. We have changed our direction to meet the needs of our students many times. Without her and her expertise, this work would not have gone forward. She is a true pleasure to work with and is a treasure as a friend.

My family has always been a source of strength and inspiration for me and I love them all dearly. As I dedicated this work to my mother, I also thought of my elder brother, David, who for all my life has been an example of conduct to me. He watched out for me as a child, blazed the trail through school for me, and continues to be my confidant and guide. Through him, I'm blessed with a sister-in-law, Mossie, who is generous and supportive, and with nieces, nephews, grand-nieces, and grand-nephews. Holidays with David and Mossie are always a lot of fun! Finally, my son, Grant, is incredibly important to me and supports me not only with love but with respect. It is mutual. We have a camaraderie not often enjoyed by a father and son. He is a deep thinker and a superb conversationalist, and we regularly share ideas and discuss their merits. His sense of humor is impeccable and always lightens my load.

From Heather: "As iron sharpens iron, so one person sharpens another" (Proverbs 27:17). If I have accomplished anything in life, it is entirely due to another person who has helped me along the way. I am the educator that I am today due to the people I have had the distinct pleasure of collaborating with throughout my career. My two mentor teachers during student teaching in 1997 will forever be part of my professional story. I fondly recall the ways both Hal Amundson and Tom Rhodes molded me during this formative time in my career. Michelle Davidson became my first collaborative partner when we both were hired to teach ninth-grade geography. Years before I would ever hear the acronym PLC, she helped me to grow immensely and held me accountable to the needs of both of our students. Rick Jacobs became my first official PLC partner. Although we did not understand all that we were being asked to do, we began the process of learning by doing each time we met, and we had a lot of fun along the way with our seventh-grade geography classes. When growth in our school created a need for a third teacher, we were blessed to add Rachael Piacine to our team. It was with this group that I grew in my craft and learned how to share responsibility for student growth with other teachers.

My only reservation in moving from the K–12 classroom to go to higher education was leaving my collaborative team. I knew that I was ready to begin working with future teachers, but I feared my days of working collaboratively would be over when I came to work at the university level. Nothing could be farther from the truth. I am forever grateful for both my Residency I team members (as previously mentioned) and my ALSI team members (Kevin Krahenbuhl, Lando Carter, Kim Evert, Angie Hooser, and Jennifer Hyde). Working in a room full of doctors can be very intimidating, but these team members have displayed the epitome of vulnerability-based trust and made working together a pleasure. I would be remiss if I did not write a special acknowledgment to Terry Goodin for being my mentor and friend these past eleven years. I sincerely appreciate your patience with me.

On a personal note, I must acknowledge my partner in life, my husband, Kris. At any time of the day or night, I know that I can count on him to support me and our family. He is a wonderful husband, father, provider, leader, and friend, and I love him dearly. My parents, Bill and Ruth Green, have always been a constant support to me as are my sisters, Beth Griewahn and Kendra Miller (also one of the best teachers I have ever known). My wonderful in-laws, Key and Shirley Dillard, have always treated me as their own child. I love and respect them immensely. Finally, I acknowledge my beautiful daughter, Hope. I am so thankful that God chose me to be your mother. Watching you grow has been one of the greatest blessings of my life.

Solution Tree Press would like to thank the following reviewers:

Dean Armstrong
Senior ELA Teacher
Melfort Comprehensive
Melfort, Saskatchewan, Canada

Becca Bouchard
Educator
Calgary Academy
Calgary, Alberta, Canada

Nathalie Fournier
French Immersion Teacher
Prairie South School Division
Moose Jaw, Saskatchewan, Canada

Erin Kruckenberg
Fifth-Grade Teacher
Harvard Community Unit School District 50
Harvard, Illinois

Rachel Swearengin
Fifth-Grade Teacher
Manchester Park Elementary School
Olathe, Kansas

Laurie Warner
PLC Trainer
Deer Valley Unified School District
Phoenix, Arizona

Visit **go.SolutionTree.com/PLCbooks** to download the free reproducibles in this book.

Table of Contents

About the Authors .... **xiii**

Foreword by Robert Eaker .... **xv**
    Clarity Precedes Competence xvi
    Learning by Doing: Exemplars xvi
    The Power of Teaming in a PLC xvi

Introduction **1**
    Thinking You Can: Self-Efficacy 2
    Shifting the Thinking in Schools: Professional Learning Communities at Work   2
    Alleviating Decision Fatigue 3
    Implementing a Problem-Based Learning Approach 3
    Making a Difference 4
    About This Book 5

PART 1: the will *and* skill 7

CHAPTER 1
Building a Powerful Partnership:
PLC at Work and PBL **9**
    Professional Learning Communities 11
    Problem-Based Learning Method 12
    A Change in Thinking 14
    Theory and Practice 15

Balance and Trust. 15

Heart, Head, and Hands 16

CHAPTER 2
Building Collaborative Willpower: Learning to Trust the PLC Process Using PBL **19**

PLC LIGHT. 19

A Trustworthy Process 25

Strength in Numbers. 29

Listening to Learn Tool. 30

Think This, Do This: Listening to Learn. 31

Think This, Do This: Integrating the Learning of Others Into Your Own Understanding 32

Tool for Integrating the Learning of Others Into Your Own Understanding . . . 33

Think This, Do This: Growing Professionally as Individuals and as a Team 34

Tool for Growing Professionally as Individuals and as a Team 35

Think This, Do This: Honoring and Trusting Your Team Members and the PLC Process 36

Tool for Honoring and Trusting Your Team Members and the PLC Process . . . 37

CHAPTER 3
Building Collaborative Skill Power: Problem-Based Learning **39**

The Roots of Problem-Based Learning 39

A Bridge Between Learning and Practice 42

The Eight Elements of the Problem-Based Learning Method 43

Problem-Based Learning Grid 48

Example Learning Grid for PLCs. 50

From Method to Mindset 51

Think This, Do This: PBL Mindset 53

PART II: PBL *training* modules 55

CHAPTER 4
Shifting From Teaching to Learning. **57**

The Four Pillars. 57

Focus on the Fundamentals. 60

Table of Contents   xi

    The Fundamentals: PBL Module Facilitator Notes..................**61**
        Think This, Do This: The Purpose of School........................ 66
        Think This, Do This: Practice, Policy, and Procedures 67
        Think This, Do This: Collective Commitments...................... 68
        Think This, Do This: Goal Setting 69
        PBL Learning Grid: The Fundamentals............................ 70
        The Fundamentals: Scene 1.....................................71
        The Fundamentals: Scene 2.................................... 72
        The Fundamentals: Scene 3.................................... 73
        Guiding Questions for the Fundamentals 74

CHAPTER 5
Shifting From Isolation to Collaboration..........................**77**
    A Systematic Process 78
    Working Interdependently......................................78
    Working Collectively on Specific Items 79
    Focus on Collaboration 80
    The Writing on the Wall: PBL Module Facilitator Notes...............**81**
        Think This, Do This: A Systematic Process......................... 86
        Think This, Do This: Working Interdependently 87
        Think This, Do This: Working Collectively on Specific Items............. 88
        PBL Learning Grid: The Writing on the Wall 89
        The Writing on the Wall: Scene 1 90
        The Writing on the Wall: Scene 2 92
        The Writing on the Wall: Scene 3 94
        Guiding Questions for the Writing on the Wall...................... 95

CHAPTER 6
Shifting From Intentions to Results..............................**99**
    Making Decisions Using Data...................................100
    Using Data to Inform 101
    Decision Making Within the System 101
    Acting With Intention: Unit by Unit 103
    Learning for All.. 103
    Learning for All: PBL Module Facilitator Notes..................... **104**
        Think This, Do This: Turning Intentions Into Actions 109
        Think This, Do This: Collectively Interpret Standards....................111

Think This, Do This: Examining Student Proficiency *112*
Think This, Do This: Focusing on Student Mastery *113*
PBL Learning Grid: Learning for All *114*
Learning for All: Scene 1 . . . . *115*
Learning for All: Scene 2 . . . . *116*
Learning for All: Scene 3 . . . . *117*
Guiding Questions for Learning for All *118*

Epilogue **121**

References and Resources **123**

Index **129**

About the Authors

Terry Goodin, EdD, is a professor of education at Middle Tennessee State University. He has both K–12 and higher education teaching experience, as well as thirteen years of corporate experience in the world of marketing. Terry's primary focus is in problem-based learning in which he has authored and coauthoring book chapters, made local presentations, delivered papers and conference presentations, written articles, conducted workshops, and designed PBL events. Since the late 1990s, he has worked with universities at the state, regional, and national levels on the design and use of PBL in a variety of disciplines and has conducted training for schools, universities, and corporations. He played an integral part in the redesign of the teacher education program in his state, using PBL. He has developed PBL events for teachers and professors to use in their practice, and he regularly consults and advises colleagues on the use of PBL. His ongoing work is in the design of PBL curricula at all levels, assisting others in their teaching practice, and envisioning the future of PBL. He received his bachelor's in general studies from Western Kentucky University, his MEd from David Lipscomb University, and his EdD from Vanderbilt University.

Heather K. Dillard, EdD, is an associate professor of education at Middle Tennessee State University. After working as a middle and high school social studies teacher for sixteen years, she has spent the last eleven years working with both undergraduate teacher candidates and graduate students in both master's and doctoral programs at MTSU. She teaches the Schools as Professional Learning Communities class in the Assessment, Learning, and School Improvement doctoral program that was designed by PLC at Work architect Robert Eaker. She has authored and coauthored book chapters, research articles, and magazine articles primarily about PLC at Work. Heather regularly presents workshops on PLC concepts and consults with administrative teams at various schools to assist in their PLC development. She received her BS in Geoscience Education, MS in Curriculum and Instruction, and EdS in Curriculum and Technology from MTSU, and her EdD in Curriculum and Instruction from Tennessee State University.

To book Terry Goodin or Heather K. Dillard for professional development, contact pd@SolutionTree.com.

Foreword
By Robert Eaker

Using the Professional Learning Communities at Work (PLC at Work) process to enhance student learning has expanded rapidly since the publication of *Professional Learning Communities at Work: Best Practices for Enhancing Student Achievement* (DuFour & Eaker, 1998). I recall that prior to writing that first book, Rick DuFour and I had many conversations about our thoughts regarding various research findings from within and outside the educational community, as well as our practical experience as experienced educators.

One of the first assumptions we agreed on is that the fundamental purpose of a school—a school's core purpose—is to ensure high levels of learning for all students. We would frequently ask teachers and administrators what they viewed as the fundamental purpose of schools. The response would often be something like: "Schools are a place where kids go to be taught." We disagreed; we saw teaching as a *tool*, not a *purpose*. We believed becoming an effective PLC requires a shift from a focus on *teaching* to a focus on *learning*—high levels of learning for all students, skill by skill. We assumed that if schools made this structural and cultural shift, they would ask fundamentally different questions and behave in fundamentally different ways.

As the book rapidly gained readers and we began speaking at PLC at Work Institutes, a frequent question emerged from educators: "What about the role of teaching? Are you saying that teaching doesn't matter?" Of course, as teachers ourselves, we knew that teaching is critically important for student success, but we saw teaching as a means to an end, not an end in itself; the end is a school's mission of enhanced student learning for every student, and teaching is the primary means for achieving this core purpose.

Deciding between the importance of learning and the importance of teaching is a false choice. In this important book, Terry Goodin and Heather Dillard convincingly demonstrate how the teaching method of problem-based learning (PBL) can be enhanced within a school operating as a PLC at Work, and the effectiveness of the PLC at Work process can be enhanced by using the PBL approach. Goodin and Dillard are experienced practitioners with both higher education experience and experience in the world of preK–12 schools, and they each have a deep knowledge base of both the PLC at Work process and PBL. These varied experiences make for an informed and practical tool for teachers—particularly teacher teams within PLCs.

Clarity Precedes Competence

Mike Schmoker (2004) often points out that *clarity precedes competence*. Mike's observation certainly applies to PLC and PBL. The popularity of both PLCs and PBL has resulted in the terms meaning widely differing things to different people. In *Mindset for Success*, Goodin and Dillard clearly define both terms and provide a solid conceptual foundation for understanding how PLC and PBL can form a powerful partnership for enhancing student learning.

Additionally, Goodin and Dillard repeatedly demonstrate how PBL, traditionally used with students, is an effective approach for enhancing adult learning. The problem-based way of thinking, which they term the "PBL mindset," can be a useful tool for developing a school's efficacy in implementing the PLC at Work process. When educators are on the journey to becoming high-performing PLCs, they will face obstacles, roadblocks, detours, breakdowns, and potholes, and at times, they will simply become lost. When a faculty has developed, and practiced, protocols for problem solving as described in *Mindset for Success*, they will naturally develop a PBL mindset, and their likelihood for a successful journey will be dramatically improved.

Learning by Doing: Exemplars

The PLC at Work process is also based on the assumption that learning is best achieved by doing. PBL is grounded in this assumption as well. People learn best by doing. But that does not mean people learn by doing just anything. They also don't learn by constantly doing something incorrectly while receiving little feedback or encouragement for how to improve. PBL, as presented by Goodin and Dillard, provides a way of thinking about how to effectively utilize learning by doing situations to enhance both student and adult learning.

To make the connection between thinking and doing, the book employs a "think this, do this" approach. Goodin and Dillard encourage readers to think carefully about why PLC concepts work in practice (think this), and they then show how to make them work in the everyday lives of teachers and administrators (do this).

In addition to explaining the why and providing the how-to, *Mindset for Success* contains high-quality examples of PBL events—examples of problem-based events that can be used to enhance learning. Providing these examples accomplishes several important things: they provide readers with exemplars of high-quality work. In addition, examples speed up the learning process—leaders more quickly learn to develop high-quality events (problems) in which to engage teachers, and teachers learn more quickly when given high-quality examples. Commonly developed PBL events can also assist teams in developing better instructional strategies, creating better formative assessments, and providing appropriate and accurate feedback to students. This can lead to improved common scoring of student work and enhance the quality of standards-based grading.

The Power of Teaming in a PLC

Collaborative teaming is the structural and cultural engine that drives the PLC at Work process. The work of teams in a PLC focuses primarily on the four critical questions of learning (DuFour, DuFour, Eaker, Many, Mattos, & Muhammad, 2024):

1. What do we expect all students to know and be able to do?
2. How will we know they are learning?

3. How will we respond when they don't learn it?
4. How will we extend the learning of students who demonstrate proficiency?

However, teams engage in other important tasks, such as collaboratively planning common units of learning and sharing ideas and materials regarding instruction. Teacher teams, working collaboratively within the PLC at Work process, enhance the power of the PBL approach. Likewise, the effectiveness of the PLC at Work process is enhanced by using the PBL approach.

The evidence is clear: schools that function as high-performing PLCs help more students learn more, more often. PBL is a highly effective teaching tool. The combination as described in this book creates powerful ideas to help more students (and adults) experience success in the complex world of today's schools.

Introduction

On April 2, 2020, when Americans and people around the world were in the midst of a safer-at-home mandate, country music superstar Dolly Parton began a ten-week video series on YouTube—"Goodnight With Dolly"—to offer hope and encouragement to children around the world (Imagination Library, 2020). In her series, Parton read storybooks from her Imagination Library. On the series' inaugural night, she chose to read a book that inspired her as a young child: Watty Piper's (2020) *The Little Engine That Could*, first published in 1930. Parton credits her mother reading this book to her as providing the thinking she needed to believe in her dreams (Martin, 2019). Growing up in a poor family in the rural mountains of East Tennessee, Parton's ability to believe that she "could" has helped her overcome many obstacles on a lifelong journey of unparalleled success.

In Piper's book, a train carrying toys and food to children across a mountain breaks down. The children need what the train is carrying, but there is no way the train can make the journey without help. In total, four trains approach the broken-down train. They have the power to help, yet only one proves to have the capacity to try. The Little Engine possesses one trait that the others do not: *she thinks she can*. She acknowledges her deficiencies—she is small and has never been over the mountain before. Despite this, she hitches herself to the train and works with all her strength to pull it. With each movement, the Little Engine chants, "I think I can, I think I can, I think I can."

Like Piper's *The Little Engine That Could*, *Mindset for Success* is about thinking, attitude, and how to persevere. Our goal is to give readers a way of thinking that will empower them to endure. It presents a practical method of taking positive actions for school improvement. If teachers are to be successful and provide a quality education for their students, they need to possess this same type of thinking. Negative thinking prevents positive actions, but positive thinking, *when coupled with determined action*, will produce the powerful and life-changing results that students need. The thoughts educators possess about their capability to pull the weight of educating students affect their ability to teach (Bandura, 1997; Donohoo, Hattie, & Eells, 2018; Waack, 2018).

There are few things in life that a person can fully control; thoughts are one such thing. This book seeks to help educators learn how to think about their thinking as it relates to the work that they must do as educators. Every student deserves to be taught by a teacher who *thinks they can* help students learn.

Thinking You Can: Self-Efficacy

"Thinking you can" refers to the term *self-efficacy*, as coined by Albert Bandura (1977). Every individual maintains a belief about his or her ability to be effective in various situations. This belief then impacts the individual's ability to try. If a person fears that they cannot be successful, then the individual is likely to see the best alternative as being to avoid the situation altogether (Bandura, 1977). This thought pattern carries over into groups, as well. The collective thinking of a group is called *collective teacher efficacy* (CTE; Bandura, 1997). Bandura (1997) explains that a group's perceived efficacy manipulates the group's beliefs in their ability levels and will in turn dictate the course of action that is ultimately taken. This thinking can be influenced positively through collaboration, a process that benefits both the team and the individual teacher. Working collaboratively as part of a team not only improves collective teacher efficacy but also positively affects the self-efficacy of individual teachers. When this occurs "teachers begin to view their own self-efficacy level based on the belief of the collective capacities of the group" (Dillard, 2012, p. 162).

The Professional Learning Communities at Work® (PLCs at Work) process provides the structure and practices for schools and districts to organize collaboratively to improve individual and collective teacher efficacy so students achieve at high levels. As Richard DuFour, Rebecca DuFour, Robert Eaker, Thomas Many, Mike Mattos, and Anthony Muhammad (2024) explain, a PLC at Work is "an ongoing process in which educators work collaboratively in recurring cycles of collective inquiry and action research to achieve better results for the students they serve" (p. 14). In a PLC, teams of teachers (grade level, course based, or vertically aligned) "operate under the assumption that the key to improved learning for students is continuous job-embedded learning for educators" (DuFour et al., 2024, p. 14).

Shifting the Thinking in Schools: Professional Learning Communities at Work

Implementing the PLC process involves a monumental shift in thinking. As educators, we need to remind ourselves that teaching is not about me—it just involves me. This typifies the attitude that the Little Engine had. She realized that the important focus of her efforts was not on her and her abilities or preparations. Her focus was on the children on the other side of the mountain. They had a need, and she was determined to find a way to meet that need. Similarly, if teachers focus their attention on themselves or their content, they are missing the point of their practice: the students in their room, and also the students across the hall, down the hall, and in all classrooms in the school. Teachers in a PLC concentrate their efforts on the learning, not on the teaching, and they do this within collaborative teams.

The need for this shift in thinking is why the union of problem-based learning (PBL) and the PLC process is a powerful one. Utilizing problem-based learning within PLCs strengthens the effectiveness of individual teachers, thus increasing the effectiveness of the team. You might be reading this book because your school or district has already begun PLC transformation and you are looking for a way to bolster that implementation—to get educators thinking in a way that eases the transition. Or perhaps you are new to the PLC process and are trying to determine where to begin. In either instance, utilizing problem-based learning helps individuals organize their thoughts while developing a course of action. While examining individual PLC components, educators can categorize their thoughts into things they know, things they need to know, and where they can go for information. Problem-based learning can provide clarity of thought to make the PLC process more doable and more effective. According to Elaine H. J. Yew and Karen Goh (2016):

> [Problem-based learning] is a pedagogical approach that enables students to learn while engaging actively with meaningful problems. Students are given the opportunities to problem-solve in a collaborative setting, create mental models for learning, and form self-directed learning habits through practice and reflection.

However, problem-based learning is not only effective for students; adults benefit from learning in this way as well. The two concepts, PLC and problem-based learning, are each incredibly strong. Together they make a powerful partnership. As we show how to put problem-based learning into action in PLCs, we reveal and explain smaller goals that will move practicing teachers and schools closer to the overall goal of increasing student learning.

Alleviating Decision Fatigue

A teacher's time is dominated by a constant need to make decisions. According to Google (Klein, 2021), teachers make 1,500 educational decisions per day. This does not account for the noneducational decisions they make. Regardless of the actual number of decisions made by teachers every day, the constant need to make decisions causes individuals to fall into a pattern of decision fatigue. During these times, individuals do not have the brain power to formulate additional decisions to problems, causing them to shut down or make poor decisions.

Tina Boogren (2018) suggests the need to counteract decision fatigue by regulating and automating various parts of the day. This includes formulating plans for basic actions that require brain activity. For instance, a teacher might automate where students place their completed assignments or how forms are turned in to the teacher. Each of these items require the teacher to make another decision that can be avoided with the establishment of an automated process.

Problem-based learning has the potential to help teachers create an automated response to decision making. When approaching any circumstance, teacher teams can utilize PBL to systematize their thinking about a problem, removing some of the bandwidth needed to think through a problem. In doing so, they can avoid the "intention trap" (intentions not followed by actions) and begin formulating plans that lead to positive results.

Implementing a Problem-Based Learning Approach

The driving force behind PBL is this: When learners are presented with a problem they can relate to, they are more likely to engage with the content required to solve the problem. According to the National Academies of Sciences, Engineering, and Medicine (2018), engagement results from "instructional approaches that focus less on the learning outcome than on a learning process organized around a question or problem" (p. 151). For this reason, PBL begins by identifying a problem and organizing learning around that problem. In this approach, the subject matter is subservient to the problem. If teachers, on the other hand, adopt a traditional, didactic teaching style, then learners don't have much agency, motivation suffers, and long-lasting outcomes are lacking. In the PBL model, learners can see the relevance of the content they are experiencing. PBL makes use of just-in-time learning, where learners receive important knowledge just at the point in time when it makes sense to have it. For example, when a team works together to process knowledge and form possible solutions during PBL, the instructor may circulate the room and observe that many learners are getting stuck at the same place. To facilitate learning, the leader may pause the entire group to deliver a short talk on an important topic.

PBL also fosters a growth mindset among learners. A mindset is another way of expressing one's beliefs and attitudes about one's abilities, and there are many examples of mindset in action. Carol Dweck (2006) has shown that some people believe that intelligence or ability is fixed and cannot be changed, while others view their abilities as changing and capable of growth. This is an important component of mindset because the fixed mindset is common, pervasive, and detrimental to learning. When teachers have a fixed mindset, their ability to teach some students may be inhibited.

A growth mindset fosters creativity (Dweck, 2006) and is integral to the mindset of an innovator (Couros, 2015). The growth mindset supports the kinds of problem-solving activities that so often involve a high level of innovation. Creative, innovative problem solvers are those who lead change and growth in society. Complex, critical, holistic thinking—that is, *problem solving*—is a goal we have for our students, and it is the foundation of PBL. As educators, we constantly strive to nourish our students' creative, innovative characteristics. When we support these beliefs in our students and espouse them in our own lives, we are furthering the development of what we call the PBL mindset: the belief, the attitude, that, with the proper education and effort, we can solve problems and thus achieve our potential and support others in achieving theirs.

This book will help individual teachers discover PBL as a new method of thinking to guide them in their pursuit of solutions. Approaching every situation with a problem-based learning mindset can help educators gain the encouragement they need to solve the everyday problems associated with teaching.

Making a Difference

Watty Piper's (2020) book *The Little Engine That Could* leaves a lot to the imagination of the reader. How long did the Little Engine try? When she first tried, did she make any movement? Did she try any new techniques with each new attempt? Why did she keep trying even though her initial efforts were unsuccessful? What caused her to maintain her belief that she could be successful?

It is highly possible that readers of this book can relate to the Little Engine. Some readers may be trying the PLC process yet are making little to no headway. Other readers may have unsuccessfully tried the PLC process. Still others may be trying to decide if they are even willing to try.

What would have happened if all the engines had decided to work together? What would be the benefits? First, the children would have received their toys much more quickly. All the engines, when working together, would have been much stronger, and their combined strength would have resulted in a quicker trip. Second, that strength of will and purpose would allow the engines to carry more weight. So, it is when teaching. Many, working together, can supply more skills and knowledge and do so in a vastly more efficient and speedier way. Truly, the Little Engine knew what the children needed and was on track to deliver. She was committed to fulfilling the mission of the trip. But what if she had not followed through? What if she was loaded and ready but had second thoughts about her abilities? She had the toys on the train, she was on the track, she was on the hill, and she thought of what children would think when they received the toys, but what would have happened if she had stopped because she thought she couldn't do it by herself? What if she had simply delayed the trip, thinking, *I'm just not ready. I think I had better wait until I'm more prepared. Maybe I'll do it next week*? But no, rather than waiting until she felt ready, she decided to go ahead and start. She had the attitude that said, "I think I can." Teachers in PLCs need this attitude as well. We must not flinch in the face of challenge. We must believe that we can make a difference and then follow through with actions that match those convictions. The time is now, the place is here, and the need is great.

About This Book

This book is divided into two parts. Part I provides the background and theory for PLC at Work and PBL, and part II presents PBL modules for leaders to use for collaborative learning about the PLC at Work process. This book is written for school leaders, professional development coordinators, team leaders, teacher leaders, and others within a school who are tasked with providing collaborative teams with training on PLC at Work implementation. It can be used with entire faculties or small groups.

In part I, chapter 1 describes the PLC at Work process along with a new way to approach the work with a problem-based learning mindset. Chapter 2 addresses the willpower needed to work as a PLC, while chapter 3 explores the skill power, or collaborative aptitude, needed to approach PLCs with a new mindset, the problem-based learning mindset.

In part II, chapters 4 through 6 each address a shift in thinking from a traditional school to a PLC and how school leaders can facilitate the understanding of this shift using Think This, Do This and the problem-based learning mindset. Each chapter ends with a module for conducting team training that leaders can utilize to introduce PLC content through the PBL process. A series of fictional scenarios introduce readers to Principal Kenneth Kindred as he leads Benjamin Franklin Middle School in the implementation of the PLC process.

Throughout this book, we apply the concept of what we call Think This, Do This to achieve practical, positive results. This simple phrase represents a challenge: If we are to prepare students for this uncertain world in which we all live, we must first prepare ourselves as educators to think in new ways and then put those thoughts into action. Think This, Do This tools presented throughout this book highlight important concepts that assist educators in reaching their goal of improving student learning. These tools present the concept that forms the basis for thought (Think This), highlight in list form what needs to be done (Do This), and then present more specifics on how to make the recommendation come to life in daily practice (Here's How). The concept reinforces the elements of the PBL mindset, helping collaborative teams of educators to develop their skills in implementing PLC concepts.

PART I

the will and skill

CHAPTER 1

Building a Powerful Partnership: PLC at Work and PBL

In blending the concepts of problem-based learning and PLC, we must first address the need for both will and skill in PLC implementation. Many schools make a commitment to PLC but lack the skill to make it work. Other schools possess the skills necessary to PLC but lack the will to enact the process with fidelity. Developing either "willpower" or "skill power" in isolation is insufficient.

The Cambridge Dictionary defines *willpower* (n.d.a) as "the ability to control your own thoughts and the way in which you behave." A further definition from Merriam-Webster says that willpower (n.d.b) is "strong determination that allows one to do something difficult." The work of teaching is difficult. Choosing to share that work with colleagues and fully interact within a PLC adds another dimension of complexity to this already difficult work. When teachers fully understand the benefits of working this way, it is easier to control actions, emotions, and urges and choose to have the will to do the work the right way. Increasing willpower is more than a simple intellectual resolve; there are neurological actions within your brain that control your will to do difficult things. As Kelly McGonigal (2012) states in her book *The Willpower Instinct: How Self-Control Works, Why It Matters, and What You Can Do to Get More of It*, "Every willpower challenge requires doing something different" (p. 14).

In the book *The Tao of Coaching: Boost Your Effectiveness at Work by Inspiring and Developing Those Around You*, Max Landsberg (2002) describes four types of workers based on their level of skill and will. When a worker has a high level of skill for a task as well as a high level of will to do the task, then managers only need to delegate tasks to the worker. This type of worker thrives when given goals to meet and the freedom to act creatively to meet them. However, when a worker has low skill and low will to work, this worker must be strictly supervised with direct guidelines given. Workers with low skill and high will to work thrive when they are coached and supported in their tasks. Conversely, workers with high skill and low will thrive when leaders instill confidence and enthusiasm in them regarding the task (Landsberg, 2002).

Researchers have used this concept to describe two types of adult learners in a PLC (Bayewitz et al., 2020). The first type has a favorable attitude about the work yet lacks training in the PLC processes. The second lacks the will to work collaboratively and therefore requires a different type of support than the first type. This is akin to the concept of failed learners versus intentional nonlearners (Buffum, Mattos, & Weber, 2009). There are a variety of factors that contribute to adult nonlearners, including PLC members who do not contribute, come unprepared to meetings, refuse to honor team norms, disengage from the work, attempt to dominate the airtime in meetings, pretend to engage while privately derailing the work, or actively reject the PLC culture (Bayewitz et al., 2020). We would contend that another factor, the inability to trust, contributes to adults becoming intentional nonlearners in the PLC process.

Trust is a skill that can be both learned and unlearned. In its absence, the lack of trust affects the will of an adult learner. When a teacher does not trust the PLC practices that they are being asked to employ, the teacher will not be willing to do the work. Therefore, it is important for leaders to help the teacher learn to trust the proven PLC practices so that their will to do the work can be increased. Muhammad Ali is quoted as saying, "Champions aren't made in gyms. Champions are made from something they have deep inside them—a desire, a dream, a vision. . . . They have to have the skill and the will. But the will must be stronger than the skill" (Wise, 2016). If that principle is attributed to the teacher, then it would behoove administrators to help teachers increase their will to be part of a PLC collaborative team. This can be enhanced by increasing their trust in the PLC process.

In 2018, the ADP Research Institute conducted a research study to determine how managers can influence the engagement level of their employees. This study included 19,346 participants from 19 countries. Findings revealed that workers who are part of a team are 2.3 times more likely to be fully engaged in their work than those who are not on a team. Additionally, when the workers had trust in their team leaders, they were 12 times more likely to be fully engaged in their work. This trust developed when team members had clarity of what was expected of them and when they felt their strengths were being recognized and appreciated (Hayes, Chumney, Wright, & Buckingham, 2019).

The study encouraged team leaders to engage in a variety of tasks, several of which relate directly to PLC at Work. First, leaders are encouraged to "engage team members in the mission of the organization" (Hayes et al., 2019, p. 50). Engaging teachers in the co-creation of a mission, vision, collective commitments, and goals (the four pillars of a PLC) supports the work of a PLC (DuFour et al., 2024). By engaging teachers in this work, the expectations of the team are made clear as shared values are strengthened, both of which are suggested by the ADP Research Institute (Hayes et al., 2019) as ways to increase engagement in the workplace.

In identifying the importance of both will and skill in the implementation of the PLC process, we must call attention to the importance of working together. Collaboration, whether it be face-to-face or via a technological link, requires explicit tools that will help teams work together well. Essential concepts like teamwork, communication, collaboration, and an active approach to problem solving must be included for new or existing PLC teams to function well. Problem-based learning presents itself as a particularly useful tool to achieve this goal.

We begin this chapter with a brief overview of the main PLC at Work concepts followed by an overview of the PBL model.

Professional Learning Communities

There was a time when educators had no preconceived notions about the term *professional learning communities*. That era has long passed. The term PLC has become so overused that its original meaning is often lost. Furthermore, many teachers have had negative experiences in schools that were practicing "PLC Lite" (DuFour & Reeves, 2016). Therefore, when leaders introduce PLCs to their faculty members, they must begin with basic information. To change the culture of any organization, a common language is essential. This book uses vocabulary from the PLC at Work process developed by Richard DuFour and Robert Eaker (1998). Many of their subsequent writings with coauthors Rebecca DuFour, Thomas Many, Mike Mattos, Anthony Muhammad, and others have been instrumental in this work.

A PLC is an "ongoing process in which educators work collaboratively in recurring cycles of collective inquiry and action research to achieve better results for the students they serve" (DuFour et al., 2024, p. 14). Educators need to understand that the purpose of their collaborative meetings is to achieve better results for the students they collectively serve. If they do not understand this fundamental purpose, the team will not be focused on the correct work when they collaborate.

The definition continues, stating that PLCs "operate under the assumption that the key to improved learning for students is continuous job-embedded learning for educators" (DuFour et al., 2024, p. 14). This portion of the definition places responsibility on both the teachers and the administrators in the building. First, the administration must establish a master schedule that allows time for all teachers to work collaboratively with teachers in the same discipline during the contractual day. It cannot be an expectation for teachers to find the time on their own to work collaboratively. Secondly, teachers need to be honest with themselves and their administration regarding their personal needs for growth. With this information, administrators should differentiate the professional development opportunities they provide according to the needs of the individual teachers. Additionally, administrators need to recognize that professional development does not have to occur outside of the collaborative meeting. For example, if a team of teachers is struggling to evaluate formative assessment results, then professional development can occur within the next team meeting as the administration supports the group in its evaluation of the most recent assessment (Dillard, 2024).

While the need for individual teacher growth is important, in a PLC, the need for teacher team growth is equally, if not more, important. Administrators should not be content until every student in the building is being taught by a high-functioning team of teachers. Working interdependently is not an inherent skill for most adults; in fact, it is possibly counterintuitive to many. Therefore, both schools of education and administrative teams must teach the skills of collaborative work (Dillard, 2016).

To comprehend the PLC at Work model, one must understand the major components: (1) the three big ideas and (2) the four critical questions of a PLC at Work (DuFour et al., 2024). We will summarize the major components as we draw from their work.

Three Big Ideas

The three big ideas of a PLC include the following.

1. **A focus on learning:** Since the fundamental purpose of school is student learning, the first big idea must be a focus on learning. This involves much more than what educators

intend for students to learn. A focus on learning involves the learning of students as well as the teachers who are leading the learning.

2. **A collaborative culture:** Learning for every single student cannot occur with teachers working alone in the confines of their classrooms. A community of educators must work in an interdependent way to ensure that the various needs of the students they serve are met.

3. **A focus on results:** After teaching of a concept has occurred, then students' understanding of the concept must be measured to determine if students have learned and to what degree. Teachers need to collectively analyze the data received from the students to determine what learning needs to happen next.

Four Critical Questions

The four critical questions of a PLC demonstrate the need for a collaborative culture to focus on the learning of each student (DuFour et al., 2024).

1. **What do students need to know and be able to do?** This question requires teachers to develop a guaranteed and viable curriculum of essential knowledge and skills in which each member of the team agrees to teach to their students.

2. **How will we know if students have learned it?** To address this question, the team of teachers must agree upon what learning looks like. Each skill that students must learn is measurable. Teachers must agree on the method of measurement they will each use when assessing their students.

3. **How will we respond when some students do not learn it?** Even with the best initial teaching, there will be some students who do not learn the material the first time it is presented. Knowledge of this fact should compel teachers to develop a plan for ensuring these students are provided additional instruction tailored to the specific learning needs of the students.

4. **How will we extend the learning for students who have demonstrated proficiency?** Additionally, a group of students will demonstrate mastery of a concept the first time the content is presented. These students should not be forced to wait for their peers to catch up to them. Rather, an extension of the concept should be presented to these students simultaneously.

As educators commit to enacting the major components of the PLC at Work model into their daily activities, they must address essential deterrents impacting both their professional theory and practice. Within each team, individual members hold a different level of skill to employ the PLC practices. Moreover, the volition of individual teachers will have an impact on its implementation. For educational leaders to enact PLCs in their schools with fidelity, they must address the will and skill of the teachers and administrators in the building.

Problem-Based Learning Method

Problem-based learning, or PBL, is a process of learning, a method of teaching, and a pattern of thought. Although we may not think of it as such, most of us already use some parts of PBL. For example, in considering the world around us, we may reflect on our challenges and tasks. From this overall view, we narrow down our focus to those items that represent problems we must address. This attention to detail reveals what we think must be done, based on some inner set of criteria. Those criteria may go unspoken, but they are present and help us to prioritize what we must do first, second, and so on. Then, drawing on our past experiences, we think about what we know that will help us decide on a course of action. If there is something that we need to know, we think about where we can find that information. We may ask someone, read something, or check online. Once we have satisfied ourselves that we know enough to make a decision, we choose a solution. Next, we enact our solution. Finally, we evaluate our results to assess our progress. If we are satisfied, we call the work "done," and move on. If we are not pleased with the outcome, we change our approach or even start over. All of this is done within a certain timeframe, whether a few minutes for a simple problem or longer for more complex situations that demand more thought.

When seen in this light, it appears that the PBL pattern of thought is simply a common and natural way of everyday thinking, and it is, but the skill of using the *complete* method to our benefit is not common at all. If it were, fewer poor decisions would be made, wisdom would prevail, and the world would be a safer and more peaceful place. It is important, then, to understand the complete method. To begin, PBL can be thought of as having three distinct characteristics: (1) a way to learn, (2) a way to teach, and (3) a way to think.

A Way to Learn

PBL applies to a variety of settings, whether in the classroom, in teacher professional development, or in administrative training. PBL is not constrained to educational applications. It goes well beyond learning in school and can be used in corporate training, or as an on-the-job component of learning a trade.

Regardless of the setting, there is a common thread that runs throughout. The primary purpose of PBL is to achieve the goal of *learning*. To accomplish this goal, PBL organizes learning around a relevant and urgent problem that needs to be solved. The problem is the focal point for learning. While the presentation of content is important, content is more easily understood when it addresses a problem. In turn, by solving an interesting problem, content knowledge becomes more relevant to the learner, and more transferable to other situations (Yew & Goh, 2016).

A Way to Teach

When used as a curriculum, PBL is particularly powerful. One important feature of the method is that students begin to take charge of their own learning and teachers function as "learning coaches," focusing on teaching students how to identify problems, search for appropriate resources, and develop solutions. As students take more control of their learning, their motivation to learn increases, a fact which lessens teacher stress considerably (Yew & Goh, 2016). Teachers who are relieved of this pressure have more time to delve deeply into the complexities of the teaching and learning interaction. Relationships are key to successful teaching, and to peer support, as well. PBL provides the benefits of social learning. Students work in teams, which means that students work collaboratively, and teachers can observe, check for understanding in more personal ways, identify individual needs, and coach students in their learning process.

The reasons for using PBL as a teaching method include that it enhances students' abilities to think and to more effectively solve problems, both in collaborative teams and independently as they learn PBL for themselves. In addition, PBL helps students to stay engaged because they can see the relevance of the content knowledge being covered. This focus on the application of knowledge can influence how students think about problems. They become more adept at identifying problems, breaking them down into smaller subproblems that must be solved, prioritizing those subproblems, and, by using the PBL process, proceeding to a workable solution. Not surprisingly, the method also improves student motivation. Success breeds confidence. As students succeed in solving problems using PBL, they are more likely to tackle life situations with confidence, hope, and perseverance (Yew & Goh, 2016).

A Way to Think

PBL also represents a pattern of thought, a mindset, that is an important part of day-to-day practice in any profession or job setting. This is the power of PBL, in that it trains an individual in ways to consider the world and address problems in a process of sensible thinking. Further, PBL emphasizes the culture of a work setting, stressing the attitudes and thinking that are part of daily problem-solving activities. On-the-job training and apprenticeships are clear evidence of the passing on of culture. When considered carefully, an apprenticeship in a trade is essentially the same as in a profession. Carpenters teach their apprentices how to cut, form, and attach the wood, using all the skills and knowledge that they've accumulated over their years of working. They also convey the important culture of the trade, such as arriving on time, organizing one's tools, cleaning up the work area, and, perhaps most importantly, defining acceptable products. Problem solving is part of everyday life on the job, and when faced with a difficult task, the experienced carpenter will show the apprentice how to approach the work, how to "think like a carpenter," and thus achieve the desired outcome. Professions and trades also have their own language and ways of communicating. Syntax and discourse reflect the context within which language is used. Vocabulary is likewise specific to the job or profession. The word *plane*, for example, may refer to a tool in the carpenter's toolbox, but to the architect who designed the house, the term will more likely refer to the flat area that forms floors or walls. To the architect, it is important to be able to calculate the surface area of the portion of a plane that is used in design.

Culture is equally as important in the professions as it is in the trades. Just as the carpenter passes on the culture of their trade, so does the architect pass on the attitudes toward work, the routines of the work, the methods that are used to approach and solve everyday problems, and the standards that determine a quality product. This is true of every profession, medical, legal, educational, and so on. In each, a pattern of thought emerges, one that reflects similar characteristics regarding problem solving and the culture of the profession. Both the trades and the professions employ PBL thinking. In both situations, the use of PBL is natural and so cultivates the PBL mindset in what we think of as on-the-job training.

A Change in Thinking

PBL can dramatically affect the professional life of the teacher, as well. The PBL mindset can develop because of regular use of PBL in the classroom, the conference room, or both. As teachers become more capable of designing PBL curricula for their students, they may begin to notice a change in their own thinking and in the ways that they interact with other professionals in the building. This is because PBL is often a collaborative process and generates projects that are naturally interdisciplinary. PBL-problem scenarios are often holistic in nature and can include elements of different subject areas. For example, in addressing a problem of pollution in a watershed area, students may act as scientists whose job it is to produce a written report to accompany a collection and analysis of scientific data. The information needed for their project would draw from mathematics, science, and English, and would be presented to a panel of experts or a county commission, along with a plan for site cleanup.

This is an example of an effective teaching method, to be sure, and is one of the best reasons to use PBL. However, the development of a PBL mindset does not begin or end in the classroom. There are many effective methods of instruction, and teachers do not have to use PBL in the classroom to adopt a PBL mindset. They can begin as a learner, experiencing the power of the process in their own professional development. Or they can use PBL to facilitate collaborative team meetings, making problem identification and solution development the centerpiece of the meeting. The effective use of PBL can help teachers to become more effective leaders, with students, parents, and colleagues. Whether experiencing PBL in professional development, using the process in collaborative team meetings, or developing their own leadership skills, teachers and administrators alike will become more comfortable with the method and the mindset.

Theory and Practice

All practice is guided by theory. Although often unstated, theory plays an important part in determining what instructional methods teachers choose, what classroom management approaches are taken, and even how professional teachers interact with each other. The term *theory* is often misunderstood as representing ideal but unrealistic insights into the field of education. In truth, a sound educational theory emerges from research into the profession and should work to tell us why a particular practice will work. For example, many teachers believe that it is important to use active learning strategies in their classrooms. Students in this setting will often apply their learning and will show evidence of increased engagement in the content being covered. This approach is grounded in the theory of "learning by doing," as developed by John Dewey (1938). Dewey, as we know, is one of the giants of educational philosophy, and his views have exerted influence on theories about learning. A study of his ideas, along with those of other great thinkers, can provide a firm foundation for educational theory, for the goals and purposes of education in general, and for why we choose particular methods to reach those goals.

If theory gives us insight into why a particular method is important, practice helps us to understand how it works in real life when the situation is less than ideal. Merriam-Webster defines *practice* (n.d.) as "to perform or work at something repeatedly so as to become proficient." Thus, it is a practical way of learning. We want to know what works on a day-to-day basis, as well as on an individual basis. What is best for our students? Schools vary significantly, and the needs of students in one setting will be different from those in another. What works in an urban school may not do so well in a rural school, and so on. Teachers quickly learn to adjust their thinking to accommodate for these differences, and to develop skills and wisdom that are related to the facts on the ground.

Balance and Trust

Under the best of circumstances, there is a balance between theory and practice. Theory helps to inform our thinking about education in general, and practice helps us to apply what we know to specific situations. It's like the principle of balance when riding a seesaw. If the weight on each end is the same, the rider can press down with their feet and rise high above the ground. A problem occurs when one rider is heavier than the other, but the heavier rider accommodates for this by adjusting so that they sit further forward on the board. They again achieve balance, albeit they are arranged differently on the seesaw.

The seesaw image can assist in understanding the Think This, Do This approach. Think This is on the left side of the seesaw. This is theory and represents what teachers and administrators think about the profession. On the right side is Do This. This is practice and represents what teachers and administrators do on a daily basis.

An overreliance on either end of the educational seesaw will result in an imbalance that hinders the performance of the system. When educators focus too much attention on theory, they risk losing attention on the day-to-day or urgent activities related to running the school. Conversely, when they focus solely on managing operations, they may find themselves unable to meet the long-term purpose of the school—to ensure the learning of each student.

Trust, a quality that can be cultivated, is critical in the balancing of theory and practice as suggested by the relative "weight" that we give to each side. If we are heavy on the theory side of the seesaw, we must learn to trust practice enough to shift our weight closer to that side. Similarly, if we find that we are placing too much confidence in practice, we should learn to trust theory, as we move closer to that side. For example, there is ample research to support the use of the PLC process in schools (Torres, Rooney, Holmgren, Yoon, Taylor, & Hanson, 2021), yet we see that there is still a need for schools to move to this model as a matter of practice. Educators who may not presently see the importance of the PLC process may be seen as being too reliant upon existing practice. To effect change, they must learn to trust the reports showing that the use of the PLC process will deliver positive results in a variety of settings. Research on PLCs proves that this act of trusting the theory, when followed by a faithful execution of practice, will yield positive and transformative outcomes for the school (Hanson, Torres, Yoon, Merrill, Fantz, & Velie, 2021).

Ralph Waldo Emerson is reported to have said, "We are what we think about all day long." From this has emerged many variants, including "You are what you think." The point is that we can, through conscious thought, impact what we become. This belief is fundamental to the process of self-improvement because if we don't believe we can do something, it is likely that we won't be able to accomplish it. The attitude reflected by Emerson's quote is never more important than in understanding the Think This side of the equation as represented by the seesaw. If teachers and administrators can train themselves to think about, and to trust, in an idea that is well supported by research and theory, then they will be much more able to move that idea to the Do This side, the daily practice that directly and positively impacts their students. This is an ongoing process, but when educators effectively connect theory and practice, they begin to change how they think and work. In so doing, they address what Pfeffer and Sutton (2000) termed the *knowing–doing gap*, that gulf between what we *think* we know to be true and what we are willing to *do*.

Heart, Head, and Hands

We often think of learning and doing as a sequential order, or process, that represents a set way to get things done. We must be persuaded that we can reach our goals (heart), which makes us motivated to learn (head), and then act (hands). PBL suggests that we not wait for these things to occur in a precise order of events, however, but rather realize that all three are happening all at once, all the time. It's okay if we "do" first, trusting that we will learn more and believe more as we go. The heart, head, and hands work together throughout. Therefore, if we believe (heart) we should effectively develop and employ a PBL mindset, we need to understand (head) more about the components of PBL itself, and we need to know how that pattern of thinking can play a role in our lives, whether we are teachers, leaders, coworkers, parents, or just friends. And we must act (hands).

Later chapters in this book provide examples of PBL in practice, along with specific instructions on how to use it to develop a PBL mindset, which in turn will support the collaborative practices teams use in PLCs.

Using PBL as part of the PLC process is a new approach. However, the partnership between PBL and PLC is a union of methods that will increase teachers' willpower to successfully tackle the collaborative processes involved in PLC implementation. The next chapter explores building collaborative willpower and trust for the PLC process using PBL.

CHAPTER 2

Building Collaborative Willpower: Learning to Trust the PLC Process Using PBL

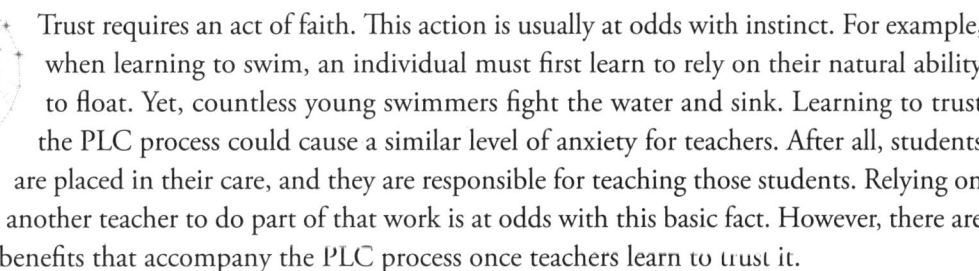
Trust requires an act of faith. This action is usually at odds with instinct. For example, when learning to swim, an individual must first learn to rely on their natural ability to float. Yet, countless young swimmers fight the water and sink. Learning to trust the PLC process could cause a similar level of anxiety for teachers. After all, students are placed in their care, and they are responsible for teaching those students. Relying on another teacher to do part of that work is at odds with this basic fact. However, there are benefits that accompany the PLC process once teachers learn to trust it.

Many schools claim to be PLCs without adhering to the basic tenets of the process in full. Richard DuFour and Douglas Reeves (2016) coined a term for these schools: "PLC Lite." A school practicing PLC Lite picks and chooses among the proven PLC practices for the ones they are most comfortable implementing. In so doing, these schools are ignoring research and evidence proving that the practices of PLCs lead to student gains. As we say in our seesaw analogy, these teachers are comfortable (heavy) with practice, but not theory. To address this imbalance, they need to build trust by moving closer to the theory side of the board. Once teachers learn to trust the PLC research in full, they can move from the futility of PLC Lite (DuFour & Reeves, 2016) and realize the benefits of what we call "PLC LIGHT."

PLC LIGHT

Educators bear a heavy load, especially in the current education climate which requires them to be accountable for the learning of every single student. Unfortunately, too many teachers struggle alone, in the confines of their own classrooms, behind closed doors, where fear can take hold. If any profession needs a light at the end of the tunnel, it is the teaching profession. Embracing

PLC LIGHT can help teachers and administrators join in bearing the burden of teaching while also igniting a passion for their work. Utilizing PBL can help individual team members grow as educators and in their ability to trust the PLC process. This union can be captured in the acronym LIGHT.

L   Listening to learn

I   Integrating the learning of others into your own understanding

G   Growing professionally as individuals and as a team

H
T   Honoring and Trusting your team members and the process

Listening to Learn

Listening effectively can be hard to do in a world so full of distractions. Teachers are so accustomed to multitasking that it may be extremely difficult for them to stop doing other tasks and simply listen. Effective listening requires an individual's full attention. Distractions must be put aside. Where appropriate, maintain eye contact. The listener should not interrupt but rather place their own thoughts on hold. The purpose of their listening should be to learn from the speaker.

Effective listening is paramount in the PBL mindset, which begins with a commitment to the other person. Alfie Kohn (1988) refers to this phenomenon as "perspective-taking," and observes that, in order to help others, we must "understand the way the world looks to them." It seems apparent that one cannot take another person's perspective in the absence of effective listening. This is sometimes hard to do, especially if the listener wants to express his or her own views. Nevertheless, it is a skill that can be learned. Beginning with effective listening is important.

Any grouping of people working together will work more efficiently when they utilize the concept of listening to learn. The PLC process requires effective listening to progress correctly toward the three big ideas that govern their work (see page 11). One example of how teachers can practice listening in a PLC meeting is as follows.

1. Collectively decide on a standard that all teachers will be teaching in the near future.
2. Individually read the standard and record thoughts as to the individual concepts and skills associated with the standard. Record any questions surrounding the standard.
3. One by one, allow each teacher to discuss their interpretation of the standard.
4. Select one person to record the details each teacher shares. Afterward, read the minutes to determine if each member's words were recorded properly.
5. Any statement recorded in error should be corrected during this review time.

Collaborative teams can use the reproducible "Listening to Learn Tool" (page 30). Refer to the reproducible tool on page 31, "Think This, Do This: Listening to Learn," to engage collaborative teams in reflection on listening within their PLC.

Integrating the Learning of Others Into Your Own Understanding

After individuals have listened to learn, they can then begin to integrate the learning of others into their own understanding. In PBL, integrating learning from each group member is an essential component of solving the problem (Yew & Goh, 2016). Since no one team member has all of the information needed to solve a problem, team members learn how to work interdependently with one another. The experience helps them to realize that integrating the learning of others is a welcome addition to their own limited perspective. This process is especially helpful when examining the four critical questions of a PLC.

Building on the actions of the previous example in the listening to learn section, teachers can practice integrating the learning of all team members during a collaborative meeting as follows.

1. After team members have read through the minutes about the standard, the group should hold a conversation about the different interpretations by the individual teachers. (This is addressing the first of the four PLC critical questions.)
2. The PLC team should discuss any areas that have been interpreted differently by individual team members.
3. If differences appear, regardless of whether they are major or minor differences, the team should come to a consensus on how the standard will be interpreted by the team as it is taught.
4. The team should then hold a conversation about how the individual skills and concepts would look if a student demonstrated proficiency. (This is addressing the second PLC critical question.)
5. From this conversation, the team should create a common formative assessment (CFA) with individual questions for each of the skills and concepts agreed on. Additionally, the team members should agree on a window of time for when the assessment will be given to each student and a time to collectively look at all of the student data collected.

Refer to the reproducible tool on page 32, "Think This, Do This: Integrating the Learning of Others Into Your Own Understanding," to engage collaborative teams in reflection on integrating the learning of others within their PLC. Teams can use the reproducible "Tool for Integrating the Learning of Others Into Your Own Understanding" (page 33) to integrate the learning of others with their own understanding. Ask team members to fill out the tool. Allow five minutes for this task. After everyone is done, ask each person to share what they learned. Allow each person two minutes to speak.

Growing Professionally as Individuals and as a Team

The brain's natural learning process, a cycle of sensing, integrating, and acting (Zull, 2002), is part of PBL, which in turn leads to the development of a PBL mindset. As the PBL mindset develops, team members understand and appreciate the importance of working together interdependently. Building on the four critical questions of a PLC, this portion of the PBL mindset assists teachers in determining their next steps. Refer to the reproducible tool on page 34, "Think This, Do This: Growing Professionally as Individuals and as a Team," to engage collaborative teams in reflection on growing professionally and as a team.

In PLCs, every individual in the school is a learner. Deeper student learning occurs as the professionals in the school build on their own learning. When team members make a habit of listening effectively, and taking action, their own professional growth is enhanced.

Continuing the previous example, teachers can begin growing professionally, both individually and collectively, during a collaborative team meeting as follows.

1. After assessing all students with the team-created common formative assessment, each team member should share his or her student data, including a discussion of individual skills and concepts for individual students rather than a list of class averages.
2. As each teacher shares, one member records information as each member looks for common mistakes and misunderstandings as well as victories. Patterns and outliers should be identified.
3. Since the methods for teaching the skills and concepts are individual for each teacher, certain teachers' methods may need to be discussed with the group. For instance, if one teacher has a higher percentage of students showing mastery in a specific skill or concept, this teacher should share their method. On the contrary, if students scored poorly on a skill or concept in all the teachers' classes, the teachers should share how they taught the skill and consider how they can learn new methods for teaching it. Often, a simple change can garner better student results. In the absence of these conversations, teachers are not able to grow together.
4. The team of teachers should then develop a list of students who need intervention and a list of students who need enrichment. These lists may be subdivided into specific types or amounts of intervention or enrichment needed based on the data. Each list will contain students from each of the teachers' classrooms. (This will begin the process of discussing the third and fourth PLC critical questions.)
5. The team should determine a method for intervention or enrichment most appropriate for each list according to each student's needs.

After teachers have addressed what students should learn, clarified exactly what learning looks like, determined how to respond when students don't learn, and how to respond when they have learned, then they will begin to grow professionally. In doing so, they honor their team members and the process because they have learned to trust team members and the process. Teams can use the reproducible "Tool for Growing Professionally as Individuals and as a Team" (page 35) to record team thoughts and growth.

Honoring and Trusting Your Team Members and the Process

The act of honoring a person requires a large measure of respect and esteem. The teaching profession inherently calls for honorable individuals to work with the most valuable commodity of society, our children: "Honor is, always has been and presumably always will be the standard by which we judge our public men and women—a form of judgment which, even in a 'nonjudgmental' age such as ours, it is scarcely possible to imagine being without" (Bowman, 2007, p. 9). One way that teachers can be honored is when individuals assume positive intentions about their work. Teachers have chosen a vocation that requires personal sacrifice with little extrinsic reward in return. Consequently, individuals should assume that teachers are acting in the best way they know how. By entering collaborative meetings with the assumption of positive intentions, each person is clearing their mind of any baggage that could potentially derail their conversations.

The act of honoring a team member in a PLC requires an individual to adhere to a standard of conduct. Honoring the PLC process involves adherence to a standard of practice. These practices have been thoroughly vetted and presented in countless articles and books (Cottingham,

Hough, & Myung, 2023; Hanson et al., 2021; Read On Arizona, n.d.; Solution Tree, n.d.a–d). Timothy Kanold (2017) eloquently explains how the act of honor in a PLC can benefit both the teacher and the students they serve:

> Our intentional effort to effectively collaborate and engage with our colleagues and to honor the covenants and agreements of a team helps to at best erase causes of inequity in our school, and at worse allows our teaching and leading life to expand its impact and find its full and realized potential. (p. 102)

Honoring the team members and the PLC process allows teachers a better opportunity to fulfill their obligation to advance the learning of the students they serve.

It is difficult to honor a team member (as well as a process) that you do not trust. For that reason, honor and trust become interlocked. The PBL mindset both requires and bolsters the concepts of honor and trust as part of the problem-solving process, in which each group member takes on the responsibility to collectively develop a solution. The act of honoring springs from, and leads to, a commitment to trust.

Refer to the reproducible tool on page 36, "Think This, Do This: Honoring and Trusting Your Team Members and the PLC Process," to engage collaborative teams in reflection on honoring and trusting team members and the process.

The analysis of student data often reveals that some students have learned information that other students have not. To properly meet the needs of all students, teachers may need to share some of their students with their team members. One team member may be working on relearning of a particular skill while another is providing enrichment. The students would then be divided among the two teachers' classrooms based on their individual needs. When a teacher shares his or her students with another teacher, they are exhibiting honor and trust for the teacher and the PLC process.

Building trust in PLC teams is foundational to the success of the team. According to Patrick Lencioni (2002), the absence of trust is the primary cause of dysfunctional teams. Lencioni recommends that teams build vulnerability-based trust to become high-functioning teams. This type of trust requires members to maintain confidence in their team members' intentions to the point that they feel safe to share personal weaknesses, deficiencies, shortcomings, and mistakes. In doing so, team members will not be concerned with protecting themselves and can instead focus on the work of the team (Lencioni, 2002).

In *Trust Matters: Leadership for Successful Schools*, Megan Tschannen-Moran (2014) defines *trust* as "willingness to be vulnerable to one another" (p. 19). The requirement for collaborative team members to work interdependently makes vulnerability inherent in a PLC, and trust becomes essential. In the absence of trust in PLCs, it is the students who are directly affected in a negative way. When teachers lack trust in one another "they are likely to be guarded in their interactions. Energy is diverted from common goals and channels into self-protection" (Tschannen-Moran, 2014, p. 149). Rather than allowing this to occur, teams should establish and maintain norms for their behavior. These collective commitments to one another should "enforce positive norms of conduct to promote and defend the norms that support professional engagement" (Tschannen-Moran, 2014, p. 150).

The absence of trust is often used as an excuse for teams of teachers to opt out of working collaboratively. However, students do not have time to wait for their teachers to learn to trust one another before they begin to work in their best interest. The time to begin the collaborative work of a PLC is not after trust is built. Rather, trust is built as a byproduct of working interdependently on a common goal. Paul Zak's research on the neuroscience of trust provides compelling evidence that the work of PLCs can enhance a teacher's ability to trust in their team members. Zak (2017) provides a list of eight behaviors that leaders must be able to manage in order to build better job performance and trust between workers. Each of these eight recommendations has direct correlations to the basic tenets of PLCs. Zak (2017) finds that workers can trust more when they:

1. Are recognized for excellence
2. Are provided with "challenge stress"
3. Are given discretion in *how* they do their work
4. Are enabled to craft parts of their job
5. Receive information broadly
6. Have intentionally built relationships with coworkers
7. Are encouraged to grow as a whole person
8. Are encouraged to show vulnerability

Honor and trust for the PLC process and the individual team members can be achieved when the team recognizes their individual and collective growth. Continuing the example from previous sections, this can occur through the following actions.

1. Distribute the individual intervention and enrichment lists to specific teachers who commit to providing the intervention or enrichment determined by the team. Deciding which teacher will be assigned to the specific groups will vary by team. Common formative assessment data may indicate that one teacher's method for initial teaching of the topic was most successful. This teacher could be the teacher assigned to the lowest-scoring group of students on that particular skill. Since each list contains students from other teachers' classes, the teacher team must determine a specific time to allow students to go to the other teachers' classrooms.
2. Team members should agree on a window of time when students will be reassessed on the skill or concept, as well as a time to collectively look at the collected student data.
3. Data analysis should be conducted using the same method described previously. The main objective is to determine student growth in the skill or concept and to determine the next actions of the teachers to facilitate further growth based on the individual needs of students.
4. The team should reflect on the collaborative process they have utilized. They should assess themselves both individually and collectively to determine how well they have listened to learn, integrated the learning of others into their own understanding, grown professionally as individuals and as a team, and honored and trusted team members and the PLC process.

Before concluding the meeting, the team should determine the next standard that members will address in a near-future unit and repeat the process in full. While the act of teaching and meeting the needs of every student will never be easy, working as a team to collectively meet the needs of students causes the workload to be manageable. Teams can use the reproducible "Tool for Honoring and Trusting Your Team Members and the PLC Process" (page 37) to record their work with team members.

To fully embrace the PLC process, a culture of "loose and tight" leadership must be embedded into the school (DuFour et al., 2024). This type of leadership means that some decisions are "tight"—everyone in the school is required to adhere to these elements. However, teachers have the authority to make some decisions about elements that are "loose." Teachers often complain that PLC requirements will remove their autonomy as trained professional educators. This could not be further from the truth. The PLC process honors each teacher's professionalism by establishing a system that allows them to thrive in the area of their greatest expertise. If teachers can learn to trust the PLC process and then decide to honor the process, the ability to trust their team members will grow naturally.

A Trustworthy Process

In an age in which information is readily accessible, it becomes increasingly more difficult to determine which information is credible. The PLC process is trustworthy because it has stood the test of time. There are decades of research in support of this work. (Visit the AllThingsPLC website to view evidence of effectiveness [https://allthingsplc.info/evidence].) In addition, after concluding over 800 meta-analyses that studied the effects of over 150,000 different school-related items, John Hattie (2012) states the three big ideas and the four critical questions of a PLC are "the most promising strategies for developing the capacity of people within our schools to assume collective responsibility for improving student and adult learning" (p. 70).

In a learning organization, working as a team is the norm (Senge, 1990). This is because the collective knowledge of the group is so much greater than that of the individuals within it. In a PLC, teaching is a team sport (Fulton & Britton, 2011) because, collectively, teachers are better able to create success for both the students and the teachers. As Zak (2017) explains, intentionally built coworker relationships support the growth of trust among team members. As the teachers learn to trust one another, the team becomes better at solving problems (Katzenbach & Smith, 1993), able to solve complex problems more creatively (Blanchard, 2009), while increasing their capacity as educators (Patterson, Grenny, McMillan, & Switzler, 2002). This growth can be explained by the concept of collective teacher efficacy.

Each teacher has a certain level of self-efficacy. When the teacher has strong convictions in his or her own effectiveness, there is an increased likelihood that the individual will develop coping methods to overcome obstacles (Bandura, 1977). These personal convictions can be strengthened when teachers are placed on a team with other teachers who themselves possess a high level of self-efficacy. Collective efficacy is equivalent to the level of each individual on the team (Bandura, 1997). Collective teacher efficacy can significantly impact student learning.

John Hattie's (2012) work asserts that of over 250 items that influence learning, collective teacher efficacy has the highest impact on students' learning. In August 2018, he recorded a message for the 2018 LEAP Conference explaining what CTE is and what it is not. This explanation directly ties to the work of PLCs. Hattie explains that CTE occurs when the teachers' collective work is "fed with their evidence of impact" (leap4principals, 2018). Simply discussing curriculum and resources is not what helps teachers become more efficacious. Rather, teachers can collectively understand how they are impacting their students when they discuss the evidence of learning (leap4principals, 2018). Hattie (2012) states:

> We need to collaborate to build a team working together to solve the dilemmas of learning, to collectively share and critique the nature and quality of evidence that shows our impact on student learning, and to cooperate in planning and critiquing lessons, learning intentions, and success criteria on a regular basis. (pp. 171–172)

An examination of the six nondiscretionary elements of a PLC at Work encapsulates what Hattie is professing. In *Learning by Doing: A Handbook for Professional Learning Communities at Work*, 4th edition, DuFour and colleagues (2024) explain six areas that administrators must tightly monitor in a PLC:

1. Educators work collaboratively rather than in isolation, take collective responsibility for student learning, and clarify the commitments they make to each other about how they will work together.
2. The fundamental structure of the school becomes the collaborative team in which members work interdependently to achieve common goals for which all members are mutually accountable.
3. The team establishes a guaranteed and viable curriculum, unit by unit, so all students have access to the same knowledge and skills regardless of the teacher to whom they are assigned.
4. The team develops common formative assessments to frequently gather evidence of student learning.
5. The school has created a system of interventions and extensions to ensure students who struggle receive additional time and support for learning in a way that is timely, directive, diagnostic, and systematic, and students who demonstrate proficiency can extend their learning.
6. The team uses evidence of student learning to inform and improve the individual and collective practice of its members.

For each of these six non-negotiable PLC practices, there is an abundance of research to indicate their effectiveness. When accompanied by Zak's (2017) research on the neuroscience of trust, it is evident that these practices also build the teachers' ability to trust in one another.

Clarifying Commitments

The use of mission and vision statements has become common practice in organizations. Often, these statements are written by a small group of leaders, disseminated to the entire work force and quickly forgotten by all. In a PLC, the mission, vision, values, and goals must have clear alignment with one another. These statements are co-created by the leadership and faculty working together. This allows all staff members to clearly understand the direction of the school and encompasses the broad sharing of information that helps facilitate trust (Zak, 2017).

For a mission and vision to become operational, the employees must examine the types of behaviors needed to meet the purpose of the organization and then agree to act accordingly. Kegan and Lahey (2001) illustrate this with a discussion of the language of complaint versus the language of commitment. When we concentrate on the language of complaint, we are focusing on things we cannot stand. But when we shift our focus to the language of commitment, we are emphasizing what we stand for. In a PLC, these commitments are developed as team norms.

For a collaborative team to begin to be fully functional, the members need to create and enforce team norms. Additionally, they must remember, "the power of collaboratively developed norms lies not in the fact that they have been written but rather in whether they are being used" (Dillard, 2019, p. 41). In so doing, the team is building trust in one another because "the single best strategy for creating a trusting environment is clarifying how members will behave and then acting accordingly" (Mattos, DuFour, DuFour, Eaker, & Many, 2016, p. 69).

Common Goals

Intelligent organizations use teams as their basic building blocks (Pinchot & Pinchot, 1993). Teams are the vehicle that move the organization into the future (Blanchard, 2009). Innovative organizations have built teaming into their culture (Edmondson, 2013). However, the mere act of working together as a team will not ensure the success of the team. Rather, team success comes when the members are focused on a common goal for which they are all mutually accountable to one another.

Inattention to results is the fifth dysfunction Patrick Lencioni (2002) identifies in *The Five Dysfunctions of a Team*. He states that one difference between a cohesive and noncohesive team is that "goals are shared across the entire team" (Lencioni, 2002, pp. 65–66). For teacher teams to have a major impact on student success, they must first establish goals that are clear, measurable, and focused on student improvement (Marzano, Warrick, & Simms, 2014). The PLC at Work process uses SMART goals for goal setting. This requires goals to be strategic and specific, measurable, attainable, results oriented, and time bound (DuFour et al., 2024). The use of this process has resulted in schools that outperform other schools with similar student populations (Williams et al., 2005).

This tendency could be a result of what Zak (2017) terms "challenge stress." When teams of teachers are working toward an achievable goal, their brains produce oxytocin which helps them to trust one another. The work of teaching all students is daunting. When goals are vague or seem impossible, the brain's natural tendency is to avoid the work. Therefore, when teacher teams establish specific attainable goals and then monitor them frequently, their trust in one another grows as does the collective efficacy of the group.

Guaranteed and Viable Curriculum

In schools that allow teachers to work in isolation to determine the answer to the first PLC critical question, What do students need to know and be able to do?, students are subjected to an educational lottery—what they learn depends on which teacher they have been assigned. In a PLC, teams of teachers answer the first critical question. According to Richard DuFour and Robert J. Marzano (2011), the process for determining what students need to know and be able to do requires teacher teams to first study the intended curriculum of a grade level or subject. The next step is to come to an agreement about which items in the intended curriculum are higher priorities than others. From this list, they should clarify the essential knowledge and skills and then establish a plan for the delivery pace of the curriculum. Finally, they must "commit to one another that they will, in fact, teach the agreed-upon curriculum" (DuFour & Marzano, 2011, p. 91). Studies show that high-reliability schools operate in this fashion (Marzano et al., 2014) because the staff "accepts responsibility for the students' learning of the essential curricular goals" (Lezotte, n.d., p. 6).

In a PLC, teachers have discretion in how they teach the agreed-on curriculum. Teachers have the autonomy to decide how they present the material. This directly addresses two behaviors that Zak (2017) lists as promoting trust in employees because the teachers have discretion in how they do their work and are enabled to craft a portion of their job.

Common Formative Assessments

After establishing the guaranteed and viable curriculum, teams then collectively develop methods to formatively assess students on the knowledge and skills of each power standard. Researchers have praised the use of formative assessments. W. James Popham (2013) states that the evidence in support of formative assessments is so compelling that the only surprising thing is "how few U.S. teachers use the process." Paul Black and Dylan Wiliam (1998) claim there is "strong and rigorous evidence that improving formative assessment can raise standards of pupils' performance" (p. 20). This is because it causes educators to "become more skilled and focused at assessing, disaggregating, and using student achievement as a tool for ongoing improvement" (Fullan, 2001, p. 71). Consequently, when used correctly, formative assessment promises to provide the largest potential gains in student achievement (Wiliam & Thompson, 2007).

The power of common formative assessments is not in making and giving the assessments, rather the benefit comes because of the collective analysis of the data. It is through this act that teachers are "fed with their evidence of impact" (leap4principals, 2018). When teacher teams analyze common formative assessment data collectively, their potential for student gains rises exponentially. This allows them a clear lens through which to view the impact of their teaching on the individual students' learning (Ainsworth, 2015). Additionally, this act leads to the type of whole-person growth that Zak (2017) attributes to increasing trust in the workplace. Data analysis of CFAs provides teachers with consistent feedback on the goals for which they are currently working to achieve, which feeds into their own growth mindset.

System of Interventions and Extensions

Once teacher teams can determine the impact they are having on the individual students, they are then ready to answer the final two important PLC critical questions. With any topic a teacher teaches, some students will master the content while other students will not. Collaborative teams must determine how they will provide both intervention and extension of the material without losing important instructional time for the next topic the teacher will teach. It is essential for teachers to guarantee that they will provide high levels of time and support for every student to succeed (Buffum, Mattos, & Weber, 2012). This is another characteristic of high-performing schools (Ragland, Clubine, Constable, & Smith, 2002; Reeves, 2006). When a "school can make both teaching and time variables . . . and target them to meet each student's individual learning and developmental needs, the school is more likely to achieve high levels of learning for every student" (Mattos & Buffum, 2015, p. 2).

Evidence-Based Decision Making

Interwoven throughout the work of a PLC is the use of evidence to base every decision on the best interests of the individual students. The main purpose of the teacher team's work is to provide "information to teachers and school leaders about their impact on students, so that these educators have the best information possible about what steps to take with instruction and how they need to change and adapt" (Hattie, 2015). The use of data not only determines which students need enrichment or remediation, but also informs the teachers of which teaching strategies are the most successful and which teachers are having the most success (Chenoweth, 2009).

Additionally, synergy is created when evidence is used to provide recognition to both the teachers and the students for meeting or working toward a specific goal. Acts of celebration, both big and small, compel all parties to continue to press toward reaching additional goals, and the level of trust across the organization is boosted in the process (Zak, 2017).

Strength in Numbers

When teams of teachers learn to work with this amount of precision, the collective will of the group encourages the individual teachers to grow stronger in their determination to do the difficult work, one of the definitions of willpower. However, will without skill is insufficient. Embracing a PBL mindset can facilitate the process of building the skills needed to effectively do the work of a PLC. The next chapter addresses this skill power.

Listening to Learn Tool

Use this list to rate your behavior at the end of the session.

1 = I did this very little   2 = I did this some of the time   3 = I did this the whole time

_____ I developed an "others" perspective.

_____ I listened without interrupting.

_____ I tracked the speaker with my eyes.

_____ I took notes when appropriate.

_____ I avoided being distracted by my own thoughts.

Topic:

Notes on My Perspective	Notes on _____'s Perspective	Notes on _____'s Perspective
Notes on _____'s Perspective	Notes on _____'s Perspective	Notes on _____'s Perspective

Mindset for Success © 2025 Solution Tree Press • SolutionTree.com
Visit **go.SolutionTree.com/PLCBooks** to download this free reproducible.

THINK THIS, DO THIS
Listening to Learn

Think This	Do This
People working together will work more efficiently when they utilize the concept of listening to learn.	☐ Develop an "others" perspective. ☐ Listen without interrupting. ☐ Track the speaker with your eyes. ☐ Take notes when appropriate. ☐ Stay focused on the speaker so that you don't get distracted by your own thoughts.

Here's How

Engage in a conversation with a trusted person about a shared interest. State that the purpose of the conversation is to practice effective listening.

As you listen, resist the urge to interrupt. Take notes about the other person's points.

Rather than being distracted by your own thoughts, make a quick note so that you can come back to it later.

After the session, take time to review your notes with the other person. Determine if your notes correctly represent what was discussed.

THINK THIS, DO THIS
Integrating the Learning of Others Into Your Own Understanding

Think This	Do This
Since no one team member has all the information needed to solve a problem, team members must learn how to work interdependently with one another.	☐ Believe that shared thoughts will create better ideas. ☐ Consider how the ideas of others add to, take away from, or change your own ideas. ☐ Bring existing ideas together to create new ones. ☐ Consider the ideas of others, especially when they differ from your own.
Here's How	
Conduct a brainstorming activity on a new topic of conversation with a trusted person. Together, choose a substantive, positive topic for discussion, one on which both members have some level of competence. The purpose of this conversation is to integrate your current views on the topic with those of the other person. Both people should have time to express their thoughts. Next, gather the thoughts and illustrate them visually. Agree on a method to record your thoughts. This could include writing ideas on a dry-erase board, individual sticky notes, a large piece of paper, or a shared screen using a variety of technology tools. The purpose is to be able to move thoughts easily from one location to another. Allow each person an opportunity to express their ideas. As each person is sharing, listen intentionally for items that confirm your own understanding and push your thinking in a different direction. Group the ideas into like categories. Add additional ideas or categories that emerge. Afterward, discuss how the other person's ideas added to, took away from, or changed your original ideas. Reflect on the integration of ideas that occurred as you discussed the topic.	

Tool for Integrating the Learning of Others Into Your Own Understanding

Topic:		
Others' thoughts that were similar to mine	**Others' thoughts that were different from mine**	**Things learned by listening to others' thoughts**

Mindset for Success © 2025 Solution Tree Press • SolutionTree.com
Visit **go.SolutionTree.com/PLCBooks** to download this free reproducible.

THINK THIS, DO THIS

Growing Professionally as Individuals and as a Team

Think This	Do This
Professional growth happens when team members listen and integrate good ideas into practice.	☐ Commit time for professional research. ☐ Commit to professional discussion about the research. ☐ Commit to listening to learn. ☐ Commit to integrating the ideas of others. ☐ Challenge unfounded ideas to ensure your professional growth.
Here's How	
With a trusted person, choose a professional topic or area in which you need to grow. Establish a future time to meet and discuss the topic. During the interim, take time to learn about the topic through reading, interviewing knowledgeable others, or conducting research. At the agreed-on time, come together to share your learning. During this session, listen to learn and integrate ideas to further your understanding of the topic. Throughout this process, reflect on how your learning and discussion affect your professional growth.	

Tool for Growing Professionally as Individuals and as a Team

Topic:	
Individual or Team Thoughts	**Data to Support Thoughts**

Individual or Team Growth

Mindset for Success © 2025 Solution Tree Press • SolutionTree.com
Visit **go.SolutionTree.com/PLCBooks** to download this free reproducible.

THINK THIS, DO THIS
Honoring and Trusting Your Team Members and the PLC Process

Think This	Do This
Collaboration is an honorable and trustworthy practice.	☐ Assume positive intentions of your collaborative partners. ☐ Show vulnerability by communicating personal weaknesses and strengths. ☐ Honor your commitments in order to earn trust. ☐ Commit to honor and trust fully so that fear doesn't overcome your commitment.
Here's How	
Continue to work with a trusted person. Agree to have a conversation about how best to work together to achieve your common goals. Identify the steps needed to accomplish your goals. Discuss your own strengths and weaknesses related to working together. Be honest with each other; be objective, not defensive. Know that it's all right to have weaknesses and to express them with someone you trust. As you move forward, talk about how you can best support one another's weaknesses while taking advantage of each other's strengths to accomplish your goals.	

Tool for Honoring and Trusting Your Team Members and the PLC Process

Standard or skill:		
Below-Target Remediation Plan	On-Target Extension Plan	Above-Target Extension Plan
Teacher students entrusted to:	Teacher students entrusted to:	Teacher students entrusted to:
Students (by name):	Students (by name):	Students (by name):

Mindset for Success © 2025 Solution Tree Press • SolutionTree.com
Visit **go.SolutionTree.com/PLCBooks** to download this free reproducible.

CHAPTER 3

Building Collaborative Skill Power: Problem-Based Learning

Teachers who are willing to collaborate, accept collective responsibility, and clarify their commitments to each other are well on their way to adopting the will necessary for successful PLC implementation. But willpower alone is not enough. For PLCs to thrive, teachers also need the "skill power" to implement the various elements involved in the process. Administrators and teachers may want to use the PLC process to further student learning, but their efforts can be frustrated by a lack of skill. This is where PBL comes into play. With its focus on problem identification, the gathering of information, and the design of workable solutions, PBL supports teachers and administrators as they progress with PLC implementation. PBL has a long and dependable history of such support, whether in instructional settings or in professional training.

The Roots of Problem-Based Learning

Problem-based learning is both an approach to learning and teaching and a way of thinking. However, it began as an instructional method that involved the application of knowledge in actual problem-solving activities as they occur in life outside of school. PBL came into prominence in the late 1960s, when Howard Barrows and his colleagues began using the method in medical schools (Albanese & Mitchell, 1993; Barrows, 1996; Hmelo, Gotterer, & Bransford, 1997; Vernon & Blake, 1993). Barrows and his team realized that the medical school curriculum was both burdensome and too complex to be covered with traditional lecture-based methods. Students were simply not able to retain the volume of information presented to them, so Barrows conceived of a new way to present material, one that focused not just on content, but on the application of knowledge to patient cases. The results of his new approach were promising, and the method quickly spread to other universities and other disciplines (Bridges & Hallinger, 1995). Today, PBL is widely used in universities in numerous disciplines and has made its way to use in secondary and even primary schools (Lambros, 2002). The reasons for using PBL as a method of instruction include that it enhances learners' abilities to think independently and to more effectively solve problems (Bridges & Hallinger, 1995; Copeland, 2000; Hallinger, Jiafang, & Showanasai, 2019). In addition, it helps learners to stay engaged because they can see the relevance of the content knowledge being covered.

The Six Characteristics of Problem-Based Learning

Just as the PLC process has defining characteristics, so does PBL (Barrows, 1996):

1. Learning must be student-centered. While students don't choose the overall goals of a course, they do have a say in how they will address information to grapple with a relevant problem. In doing this, they begin to realize that learning is a process, and that they can master this process and use it effectively in many different settings. The goal is for them to understand "how to learn," an insight that will serve them well throughout life.

2. Learning occurs in small student groups that address topics in modules. Participants learn to interact with other learners and with the facilitator in a more intense manner, which builds the skills needed for effective teamwork.

3. The role of the instructor is fundamentally changed from being the giver of information to being a facilitator or coach in the learning process.

4. All learning is organized around a central problem. Content is engaged as a means of solving the problem or problems that form the motivation for learning.

5. The problem serves as a means of building problem-solving skills. Various problem-solving strategies may be employed at this point.

6. It is expected that new information is gained through self-directed learning by students. (pp. 5–6)

The timeline of PBL development reflects these foundational points, as well as an evolution of thinking and an expansion of the method into many different fields. As it grew in popularity, the core concepts began to be more clearly defined. Early PBL practitioners believed that as students engaged with the problem and with each other, they developed the ability to access relevant information, present it to their fellow group members, and discuss, debate, and effectively apply it to the problem. The model continued to develop and expand to other applications, and a new understanding of the process began to emerge. In an important contribution in the mid-1990s, Edwin M. Bridges and Philip Hallinger (1995) advanced the understanding of problem-based learning by asserting that the method rests on a different set of assumptions than traditional educational efforts do. Rather than viewing "teaching as the transmission of knowledge and learning as an acquisition of that knowledge," these researchers offered the following in their description of PBL:

> PBL rests on an entirely different set of assumptions. PBL proponents assume that learning involves both knowing and doing. Knowledge and the ability to use that knowledge are of equal importance. Program designers also assume that students bring knowledge to each learning experience. Moreover, PBL adherents assume that students are more likely to learn new knowledge when the following conditions are met: (1) their prior knowledge is activated, and they are encouraged to incorporate new knowledge into their preexisting knowledge; (2) they are given numerous opportunities to apply it; (3) they encode the new knowledge in a context that resembles the context in which it subsequently will be used. (Bridges & Hallinger, 1995, p. 5)

The characteristics of PBL, fostered by the medical model and later adapted by researchers in educational leadership (Bridges & Hallinger, 1995; Goodin, Caukin, & Dillard, 2019), include the following:

> (a) the starting point for learning is a problem, (b) the problem is one that students are likely to face in the future, (c) subject matter is organized around problems rather than around disciplines, (d) students take major responsibility for their own instruction and learning, and (e) most learning occurs within the context of small groups rather than lectures. (Bridges, 1992, pp. 5–6)

Because of this, instructor roles changed significantly as well, shifting away from didactic instruction. In PBL, teachers take the role of facilitators, or guides, rather than being the "givers of knowledge" (Barrows, 1996).

Problem-Based Learning in K–12 Education

PBL began to find its way into K–12 schooling, where it produced the same benefits as it did in post-secondary education. In *Problem-Based Learning in K–8 Classrooms*, Ann Lambros (2002) states, "PBL creates opportunities in the classroom that traditional approaches simply do not" (p. 4). The most significant, she says, is that the students experience a heightened sense of relevance regarding their learning. Because problems are drawn from the real world, students become interested and stay motivated to reach a solution. They tend to "work longer and harder" because they are excited about the problem. In addition, Lambros (2002) maintains that they begin to show signs of developing a "process for lifelong learning" (p. 4), an important outcome that agrees with the research done on the Jasper Woodbury curriculum project at Vanderbilt University (Bransford, 1997) and in the work of Cindy E. Hmelo, Gerald S. Gotterer, and John D. Bransford (1997). Edward H. Seifert and David Simmons (1997) began using PBL in high school settings, where they identified similar characteristics of the instructional unit. They concluded that the PBL instructor should do the following.

1. Identify a problem that students would consider useful.
2. Place the problem in an authentic context for the students.
3. Structure the subject matter around the problem as opposed to the discipline.
4. Have students take responsibility for their learning and problem solutions.
5. Create collaborative learning groups.
6. Require all students to demonstrate their learning by creating a product and making a public presentation.

In a study that focused on low-income urban minority students, P. R. Gordon, A. M. Rogers, M. Comfort, N. Gavula, and B. P. McGee (2001) found that students' behavior improved through the use of a PBL project. Behavior ratings were significantly better, with the study reporting a 20 percent improvement for the sixth-grade year and a 17 percent improvement for the seventh-grade year. Results of the study also showed that students felt positive about the use of the PBL project and that they enjoyed and valued this approach. They most liked being responsible for their own learning, and strongly advocated the continued use of PBL in their school. In a finding that portends significant contributions to PLCs, the method was credited with improving "collaboration among learners," as well as increased motivation, as students became more interested in the problem under study (Maxwell, Bellisimo, & Mergendoller, 2001; Stepien, Gallagher, & Workman, 1993). Finally, there are studies that report that PBL experience results in better retention of key concepts and learning skills, and better performance in school. Gordon and colleagues (2001) found that the middle school students in their study who experienced the problem-based curriculum also performed better on their report cards, as compared with a control group who did not receive the enrichment. The use of PBL has also been shown to improve creative problem-solving skills in elementary, middle, and high school students, over time (Clouse, Goodin, & Aniello, 2016; Goodin, 2003).

PBL fosters interdisciplinary learning because the learning is centered on a problem as opposed to being based on the premises of a particular discipline (Walton & Matthews, 1989). This assertion is supported by the fact that PBL scenarios are organized around the solution of a problem. Accordingly, students tend to draw from many different sources in the process of reaching a solution (Stepien et al., 1993). These sources are the disciplines, but also represent an inquiry into various other references. In addressing the field of educational leadership, Bridges and Hallinger (1995) state that "problem-relevant knowledge comes from a variety of sources: the disciplines, the relevant expertise and practical wisdom of practitioners, the policies and practices of the local district, and the students themselves" (p. 8). The same may be true for all levels of PBL implementation (Maxwell et al., 2001).

The roots of PBL are deep and well established. The method has grown in popularity and its usage has spread to encompass an ever-widening circle of practice. With PBL, teachers begin with an interesting problem, thus creating a "hook" to entice learners to engage with content to solve the problem. Teachers first use realistic scenarios to frame the problem and encourage inquiry. Once students are engaged, and only then, teachers expose students to resources that contain the content. Students are allowed to inquire, make connections to relevant content, and experiment with possible solutions. The teacher's role then changes from information giver to learning coach. During the problem-solving experience, teachers provide feedback and coaching to support learning. Students create solutions in the form of "products" that are used in life, and often these products are judged by outside experts in a process that extends learning beyond the bounds of what we think of as a summative assessment.

A Bridge Between Learning and Practice

Problem-based learning is a particularly powerful approach to teaching and learning because it takes advantage of natural motivators. By considering problems in contextual, holistic scenarios, learners begin to understand how information relates to life situations. When done well, PBL becomes an effective bridge between content and practice.

PBL has a history of working with simulations, where learners experiment with proposed solutions in fictional situations. This practice is reflected in various forms of professional training, such as aircraft simulators for pilot training, mock trials for law students, and medical manikins for physician training. Authentic PBL scenarios allow students to "try out" several possible solutions to authentic PBL scenarios and actual problems to gain experience that they would not otherwise get until they begin to practice. When using PBL in PLCs, we envision an emerging PBL model that we refer to as *dynamic PBL*, where actual problems of practice are used as part of the curriculum. Learners in this model do not experience a simulation but rather apply PBL to situations found in the present. It is important for learners to gain problem-solving skills, and

PBL lends itself well to this application. Further, the regular use of the method will lead to the development of the PBL mindset, which then becomes a habitual practice for learners as they make the transition from class to life.

The Eight Elements of the Problem-Based Learning Method

When used as an instructional method, PBL events generally take the form of modules or units. While they may be of different lengths, each PBL module is composed of similar elements. Bridges and Hallinger (1995) identify eight key elements.

1. Introduction
2. Problem
3. Learning objectives
4. Resources
5. Product specifications
6. Guiding questions
7. Assessment exercises
8. Time constraints

If a project is missing even one of these essential pieces, it is not a complete PBL project and may not produce the desired learning as a result.

The following are brief descriptions of each of the eight elements. It should be noted that these are the curricular elements that comprise PBL. We cannot emphasize enough that the use of PBL, *either in teaching practice or as a learner*, supports the growth of the PBL mindset, and it is this new way of thinking that is so essential to the use of PBL to support more effective collaborative teams in PLCs.

Introduction

The introduction is the *why* of the PBL project. The PBL introduction places the problem in context. By providing big-picture information, it lays the foundation for the problem and piques learners' interest to know more. After the introduction, learners should begin to see how even small-scale problems reflect larger issues.

When using the PBL method to support PLC implementation, the introduction could take on a variety of forms, depending on the context of the problem. Examples might include a discussion among team members about the history of the school, the population it serves, and current issues in education related to those populations. Activated by this context, collaborative teams would be ready to relate to a problem of practice in their school, whether in the school as a whole, in teachers' classrooms, or at the grade level.

Problem

The problem learners focus on in the PBL project must be relevant to the current situation. It must be engaging and worthy of time. This means that it needs to require both *careful* and *urgent* consideration. The problem situation should not be clear-cut but should instead be murky enough to require serious thought. Likewise, there may be several parts to the problem. Life scenarios are often complex and may need to be addressed in parts. This is an important characteristic of PBL problems and one that can be uncomfortable because there seems to be no clear, easy answer. Learners often find it difficult to break larger problems into manageable parts, or subproblems, but this is a useful skill that emerges because of the PBL process. As each of the subproblems is identified and solved, learners find that this learning can inform the understanding of and solution to the larger problem. This results in an increase in the skill of critical thinking.

In a PLC, the problem is framed in the context of the school as a system, addressing problems at the school level or at the level of individual classes, where teachers approach learning "kid by kid, skill by skill" (Eaker & Keating, 2015). To use the previous example, a PLC might consider the achievement gap that is present in their own school. That problem is brought to the team level as members analyze the results of the most recent assessment. The team would describe the situation and include as many facts as possible in that description. They wouldn't have to fully analyze the facts but should state as many as they can to paint a clear, accurate, and robust picture of the problem. This practice of mutually defining problems helps the team to think of possible solutions, which are then addressed during the rest of the PBL process.

Learning Objectives

As with any curriculum, learning objectives are vital to success. Problem-based learning encourages teachers to develop clear learning objectives for modules in the classroom. The objectives are typically layered from concrete to abstract, from simple to complex, like Bloom's taxonomy (Armstrong, 2010; Bloom, 1956) or another such model. Unlike traditional curricula, the PBL approach stipulates that these module-level learning objectives are not shared with students, since doing so would reveal the "correct answers" to them and the goal of PBL is to encourage students to take charge of their learning. The objectives are present in the background, and teachers use them to provide direction, gather resources, and arrange activities that learners experience. When done well, the process allows teachers to manage the "solution space" (Hmelo et al., 1997; Vye, Goldman, Voss, Hmelo, & Williams, 1997) within which learning takes place, thus ensuring that objectives are met.

In PLCs, learning objectives are not stated in the same form as in the classroom, but they are present nonetheless, and take the form of learning tasks that team members develop collaboratively and take on individually as part of their professional practice. At the heart of this process is the PBL Learning Grid, a graphic organizer used to visualize the collaborative efforts of the team (see reproducible on page 53 for more details). The PBL Learning Grid exercise is action-oriented in that collaborative teams in a PLC establish and choose learning tasks for themselves. The learning tasks focus attention on the central purpose of a PLC, which is student learning, and provide direction as to specific *actions* required to achieve that purpose. This connection between purpose and action is critical to keeping the focus on the goal of solving problems of practice. The question becomes, "What are we trying to learn, and how are we improving our practice through our learning?" This PBL question supports the four critical questions of a PLC: (1) What do we want students to learn? (2) How will we know if they have learned it? (3) What do we do if they haven't learned it? and (4) What do we do if they have learned it? (DuFour et al., 2024). For example, when a collaborative team is considering the achievement gap for the most recent standard students have been learning, they might have an objective to identify common mistakes among their students around this content and design a method to address the inconsistencies.

Resources

PBL requires the use of credible resources to inform solution development. This is true with any instructional method, but with PBL there is a greater level of student control over learning. That doesn't mean that the project should be allowed to go in just any direction. Some structure may be needed. In a classroom setting, either the teacher provides resources or students research and discover them. The decision of whether to provide resources is largely based on an understanding of the learner regarding current knowledge, the need for support, and maturity in terms of being a self-starter. This phase of the project is done in a modified jigsaw process, where students take responsibility for one of the topics, conduct research on it, and return to the team to educate others on it.

In a PLC, teachers assume positive intentions of one another. Teachers are mature and motivated to adopt an attitude of collective inquiry. This involves individual teachers locating resources that will assist the whole team, which is similar to the classroom jigsaw method. In addition, different levels of administrative support are needed, depending on the needs of the team. Some teachers may not need any initial support and may discover resources based on their understanding of the problem the module is addressing. In other cases, teachers may lack the requisite knowledge and may need it to be supplied as groundwork for the upcoming team meeting. This knowledge can be supplied in a few ways; for example, each team member may be asked to supply information for the first meeting from their area of expertise, or the administration may supply readings or other sources of information.

To continue the previous PLC collaborative team example, after the team has identified the common errors students made on the most recent assessment, members must then begin a deeper study of the standard in question. First, they must determine that each team member holds the same understanding of the parts of the standard. The standards document becomes a resource the team uses. Next, the team may begin to research the parts of the standard using textbooks and ancillary documents, other teachers in different schools, internet searches of related documents, and so on.

Products

In the classroom, the products of a PBL experience should reflect what would occur in the real-life situation that inspired the module. For example, a PBL about power blackouts in a particular state might naturally call for the design of a solar farm. Course materials would be organized by the instructor in such a way that students would experience the intended content about the power supply, the grid, environmental impacts, and so on. PBLs can occur in any discipline or subject area. In every case, the required products must correspond to specific learning objectives in such a way as to ensure that the whole module works together to achieve its overall purpose.

In a PLC, the product is also related to the learning objectives. The difference is that the collaborative team in a PLC will set those objectives, or tasks, for themselves. The team will have identified the problem and worked together to define what the product should look like. It will be practical and will represent a solution to the problem. Continuing with the previous collaborative team example, the team members will have identified the common errors students made in the assessment. Once identified, the team must address each error for each student. This may require reteaching the material to some students in a different way from how it was first delivered. Students may need to present their understanding of the concept in a different form. The product will vary with each case. Whatever form it takes, the overall objective for the product is that it addresses the problem statement.

Guiding Questions

Sometimes in a PBL experience, students get stuck in their thinking and need a gentle nudge to get them started again. In this case, open-ended, reflective questions supply the needed push. These questions are called *guiding questions*, rather than *leading questions*, for a reason. They reflect the role of the instructor as a learning guide, not as the leader of the learning. Students are in charge of their learning to the extent possible. Guiding questions clarify the problems the group is discussing or describing. Process-oriented questions are another form of guidance that instructors use. Problem-solving teams often need to be reminded of where they are in the process. For example, students in PBL experiences frequently confuse analysis with facts. They may make inferences from the problem scenario and need to be prompted to consider the nature of their inference. Is it a fact, or an analysis? Either is acceptable, but students must learn to distinguish the difference if they are to master a level of critical thinking. When teachers guide students in the process of learning, they are assisting them to think carefully and in an organized manner.

PLC teams can also benefit from guiding questions that assist them in the problem-solving process. If team norms call for a culture of interdependence and mutual accountability, there will likely be a sense of respect and shared input. In this environment, it is natural, even expected, for any member of the team to question whether or not the group is on track toward the solution of the mutually defined problem. More experienced team members and leaders should monitor and remind the group of where they are in the process of solving the problem. In the PLC at Work literature, the four critical questions drive the work of the team (DuFour et al., 2024). Throughout the year, as teacher teams address new standards, team members should constantly answer the four critical questions: What do we want students to learn? How will we know that they have learned it? What will we do for students who have not learned it? and What will we do for students who have learned it? (DuFour et al., 2024). These are the process-oriented questions that are always appropriate in a PLC. Additionally, the team members should dig deeply into their collaborative pursuits to help all students learn at high levels. They should welcome opportunities to push the group's thinking and never avoid *What if?* questions or asking about a counterpoint for a given topic. Collective inquiry and action orientation are two of the essential characteristics of a PLC. When collaborative teams are relentlessly questioning the status quo, they will not rest until they have tried every possible method and questioned every single decision made by the team. This pursuit has a much higher potential to find solutions to every problem than resting on the merits of "how we have always done it."

Assessments

Every PBL project must have a way to determine success or failure. This can take varied forms depending on the nature of the learning involved. Assessments can be formative or summative evaluations of the product. In the classroom, during the problem-identification phase, students produce work that can be evaluated. While much of the work is done in groups, there are points of individual evaluation possible as well. The PBL Learning Grid reflects the thoughts of the group, and the teacher can interact with the group as a whole or get a sense of each student's progress in areas such as comprehension or critical thinking.

In the classroom, students take on the role of researcher during the last phase of the PBL session, when the PBL Learning Grid is completed. They conduct research in a modified jigsaw approach, where they accept a topic, gather information about that topic, and report back to the group. The report is in the form of a research brief that each group member will receive. This is another example of an important point where evaluation should take place. Teachers evaluate these reports for content, format, writing, and presentation skills.

Summative assessments can be traditional objective tests but usually take the form of product presentations, where student teams present their solutions before their classmates or outside experts from the field. These presentations are also useful as formative assessments that move students forward in terms of continuous learning. Experts can give feedback on the backstory, which educates students on what they got right and what they should have considered.

In a PLC, to avoid confusion, *assessment* could more accurately be called a *gauge* of teaching success and will ultimately be determined by whether students have learned. If learning occurred for all students, then the solution to the problem was successful. However, not all problems that PLC teams address will be as easy to assess. When the problem is procedural in nature, the success might be measured by whether the procedure sets the team up to better help students learn. For instance, nonproductive team meetings can be eliminated when team members formulate and then honor team norms. If the team norms are allowing the team to be more successful in their meetings, then the product of team norms would be measured as successful.

Time and Schedule

When PBL projects are planned, it is important to consider how much time is needed. In the classroom, PBL modules can be designed to take a single-class period or extend across a week, a grading period, or even a whole semester. The ingredients of the module are still the same, no matter the time involved. For example, a short module may be constructed to teach a single concept, while a longer module is designed to integrate multiple concepts into a constructed project. Teachers who use PBL in practice are encouraged to develop a timeline for activities as part of their planning.

Problem-based learning complements the work of a PLC because of its focus on a team process for identifying and solving problems. Collaborative teams in PLCs realize the importance of an action orientation. Teachers only have their students for a year, and they know they must take actions that will positively impact student learning. The forward motion of PBL allows collaborative teams in PLCs to avoid "analysis paralysis," a situation in which teachers become locked into thinking about problems rather than making decisions and moving forward. PLC teams use SMART goals to identify next steps (DuFour et al., 2024). These are time bound, and progress is expected to be made within a certain timeframe to coordinate well with the selection and implementation of the PBL product.

These eight elements are simple enough. The important point is that each is essential to PBL. In the classroom, a teacher may design a beautiful PBL module, with an interesting problem, and a fascinating product, but if it isn't attached to appropriate learning objectives, it is likely wasting precious instructional time. It might be lots of fun, but what are the students learning? Likewise, in the PLC collaborative team setting, we must be sure that our thinking revolves around the problem in ways that bring out useful solutions that matter in our practice, which is to help students learn more effectively. While employing PBL, we must also keep in mind the four critical questions of PLCs: What do we want students to learn? How will we know if they've learned it?

What do we do if they don't learn? and What do we do if they do? These questions are key to the successful application of the elements of PBL to the PLC setting.

Problem-Based Learning Grid

Central to the problem-solving process is the ability to identify problems and possible solutions. Problem-based learning makes use of a brainstorming document called the PBL Learning Grid to frame thinking by organizing information into the categories of facts, information needed, analysis, and research. Figure 3.1 shows the grid, which states the problem or solution in the center surrounded by four quadrants with the following questions.

1. What do we know?
2. What do we need to know?
3. What do we think we know?
4. What will we research to find a solution?

When teams use the reproducible "PBL Learning Grid," they begin in the top left corner recording their thoughts to the question, "What do we know?" This box records facts only. If an individual makes a claim that is not a fact but rather is based on intuition or an analysis, that item is recorded in the bottom left box. As the discussion continues, the team will then begin to address items that are unknown that could aid in the solution to the problem. These items are added in the top right quadrant to answer the question, "What do we need to know?"

Teams should spend time working in the bottom left box to frame the problem statement. Too often, teams never fully understand the problem they should be addressing. Consequently, their actions are not effective. Once they have thoroughly determined the problem they need to address, they will record it in the center of the grid. At that point, the team is ready to decide on a list of researchable tasks to help find a solution to the problem. The team should record items they can learn more about in the bottom right corner of the grid.

The PBL Learning Grid can be used in collaborative meetings to promote an organized, thoughtful, sensible approach to thinking. Using this model is so important that we contend that the use of the grid is the key to developing the PBL mindset. It helps to have the grid visible to the whole team during a PBL session so that they can work on it together. It can be projected on a screen or written out on a whiteboard or large poster paper. When using the grid, team leaders should take the time to make sure that the team is sticking to the process.

When teams are first introduced to a problem scenario, they should consider the facts of the situation, making sure to glean all the information available from the scenario. There is a wealth of data available about students, for example, and that information can lead to an extensive list of facts about those students. A collaborative team in a PLC would need to focus attention on understanding the basic facts that the student data present. They would list all the facts at their disposal in the top left quadrant of the PBL Learning Grid.

Only after organizing all the facts should a team begin to think about the problem or problems that are revealed there. As they do that, they will come upon gaps in their knowledge. At that point, they move to the top right corner of the PBL Learning Grid. They will make a list of

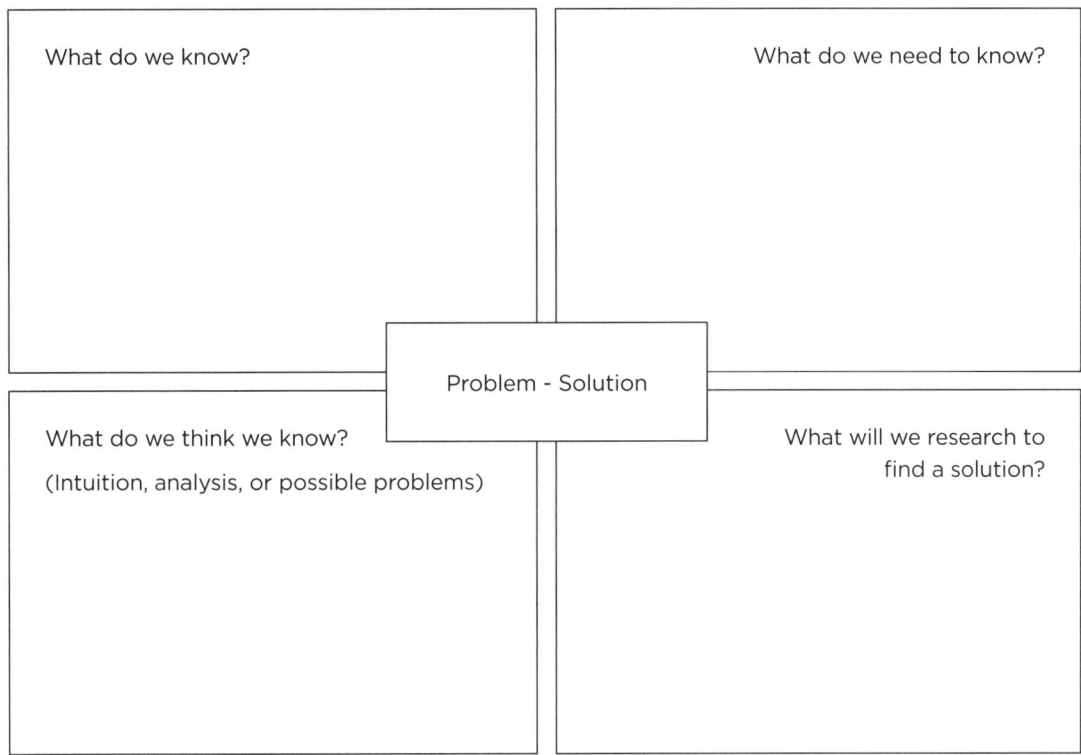

FIGURE 3.1: *PBL Learning Grid.*

*Visit **go.SolutionTree.com/PLCbooks** to download the free reproducible version of this figure.*

things that they think they need to know to make progress toward a solution. The information needed will address the knowledge gaps that they agreed on.

This process brings about some interesting thinking. To identify the gaps in knowledge, the team will have to consider the nature of the problem itself. They will need to start working on a statement that reflects the problem. To do this, they drop down to the bottom left section, where they will begin to make sense of the facts and gaps in knowledge. They may have an insight into the problem based on personal experience, or they may have some information to add to the discussion. One caveat: At any time, anyone can state what they "know" to be true. However, their knowledge must be verifiable by some external source. By requiring support for ideas, teams can reduce the possibility of error, including "groupthink," where everyone agrees with an erroneous belief or refuses to take a stand because of peer pressure. Completing the PBL Learning Grid exercise will gradually reveal what the group considers to be the real problem. At this point in the process, they will form hypotheses about the problem and possible solutions. To move forward, they will naturally adjust the items in the "What do we need to know?" corner of the grid.

After teams have filled in the first three quadrants and have formulated a problem statement, they need to have a way to do the research necessary to inform their judgment about the problem. They need to know whether to confirm or refute their analyses and subsequent problem statement. This is where the research corner comes into play. Using the list of items in the top right quadrant, the team will make a list of tasks in the bottom right quadrant. It is common for some items "we need to know" to be combined into one researchable topic or for irrelevant or redundant items to be eliminated from the list and therefore not researched. The result should be a clear list of items that are essential to the group's understanding of the problem and its possible solution. At this point, the group will distribute the learning tasks among the members in the form of a jigsaw, where each member will research their tasks with the purpose of coming back together to discuss the information and form new understandings of the problem and its solution.

Collaborative teams that are new to PBL should resist the temptation to jump around on the PBL Learning Grid, at least until they have gained enough experience to be comfortable with the process. More experienced PBL practitioners can make those leaps, using the grid holistically. This kind of "expert thinking" is useful in saving time when considering a problem and is an indicator that the practitioner has progressed in using PBL enough to have attained the PBL mindset.

Achieving mastery with PBL is not necessary for implementation, however. Even novice teachers, or those with little experience with PBL, can thrive by applying PBL with fidelity and diligence. The use of the PBL Learning Grid brings an element of discipline to the problem-solving activity because using it demands that all the blanks are filled in during the thought process. Using it consistently will benefit all concerned. PLC teams must work collaboratively through the PBL Learning Grid, and that encourages the attitudes of collaboration and mutual accountability that are important to having successful PLCs.

Example Learning Grid for PLCs

Often, teachers will have a problem but do not know how to define it. More likely, what they term as a problem may be the symptom of the problem. This is why it is so important to conduct a root cause analysis. For example, in a PLC, a team of teachers may look at the results of an assessment and recognize that a certain number of students failed. One teacher, Mrs. Pine, may realize that 30 percent of her students failed the recent benchmark assessment on the Pythagorean theorem. She could say the problem is that these 30 percent of the students did not study for the test, thereby placing the sole responsibility for their failure on the students. If this is the case, Mrs. Pine might feel satisfied with her diligence in presenting the information and simply wash her hands of the 30 percent who chose not to prepare. However, that would be a disservice to the 30 percent who failed. Working in a PLC requires teachers to look at data student by student, skill by skill (Eaker & Keating, 2015). After all, 30 percent of one hundred students is thirty students who have not yet mastered the Pythagorean theorem and therefore are not yet prepared to move on to the next mathematics concept.

When Mrs. Pine compares her scores with her teammates, Mr. Jacobs and Ms. Green, she might discover that the students in their classes also had similar results. Therefore, ninety students need to be retaught. This should spark the group to begin asking why they were not proficient. The fact that ninety students failed the test is not the problem—it is the *visible* symptom. Utilizing the PBL Learning Grid can help teachers with a root cause analysis of the problem.

The PBL Learning Grid requires team members to first ask, "What do we know?" Working collaboratively, Mrs. Pine, Mr. Jacobs, and Ms. Green begin recording what they know. Initially, they would record the fact that 90 students failed the assessment. The second question on the PBL Learning Grid asks, "What do we need to know?" This group needs to know why the students failed. The teachers must dig into the assessment. As they dig, they might notice that most of the students missed question number 2, and they record that detail in the top left quadrant. This leads to the next question of why the students missed question 2. Since this was a multiple-choice question, they might notice that most of the students who missed question 2 had marked answer choice C rather than the correct answer of D. The teachers might ask, "Why are the students choosing C?" By directing their attention specifically at the actions of the students, they might discover that answer choice C was worded in a way that could easily confuse a student if it were misinterpreted. With that discovery, Mrs. Pine re-examines the question from the perspective of the thirty students in her room who failed the assessment she helped to create with her colleagues. Figure 3.2 shows the PBL Learning Grid this collaborative team used in their root cause analysis of their problem.

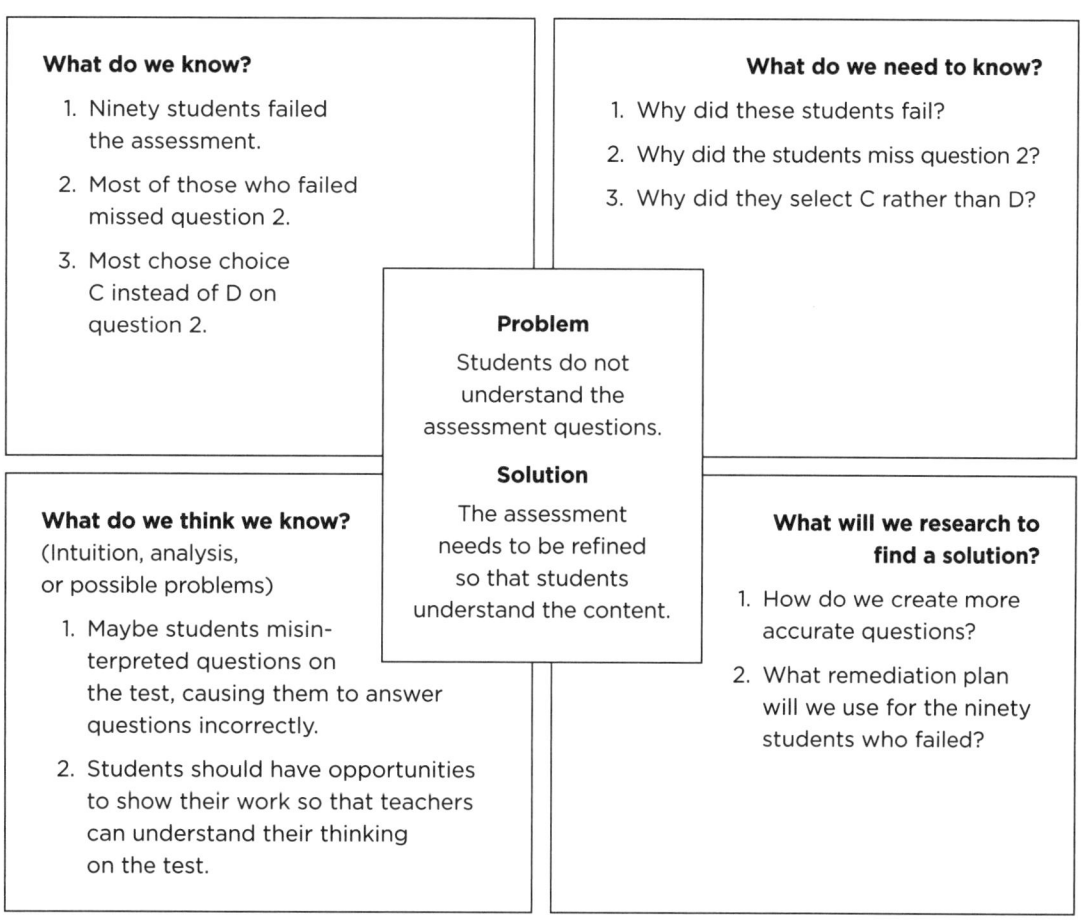

FIGURE 3.2: *Completed example PBL Learning Grid.*

From Method to Mindset

We began this chapter with a call for leaders to coach teachers who perhaps have low skill but possess high will. This requires commitment and support from school leaders. These committed educators need to have a system in place to augment the powerful PLC concepts and to ensure that those key concepts are put into practice. Problem-based learning, with its associated PBL Learning Grid, is such a system. The grid is an effective tool for managing thinking, and it is also effective for managing accountability. A completed grid shows, quite clearly, the thought process, problem identification, and solution paths of collaborative teams. This opens the door for the next step, measuring the results. Collaborative teams can be empowered to make changes in their practice to reflect the increased knowledge that is gained by using PBL. In turn, leaders can easily monitor the activities of collaborative teams by examining the completed grids.

Committed, caring leaders have an incalculable impact on the practice of educators in PLCs. Teachers often extol the virtues of such leaders, and when they know that they have such support, they are more able to both implement and sustain their PLC efforts. Problem-based learning can thrive in such a culture as this, and the use of the method, with its focus on collaboration, learning, and student results, will in turn reinforce the benefits of the PLC process. Problem-based learning leads to a PBL mindset, and by embracing the PBL mindset, educators can increase their skill in implementing the PLC process.

The "Think This, Do This: PBL Mindset" reproducible will help you reflect on how to implement the PBL method in the work of your collaborative teams. In part II of this book, you will find the PBL professional development training modules to use with collaborative teams in your PLC.

THINK THIS, DO THIS
PBL Mindset

Think This	Do This
Regular use of the PBL method will lead to the formation of the PBL mindset when approaching problem scenarios.	☐ Use PBL as a part of your professional practice. ☐ Use the PBL Learning Grid to record your thoughts. ☐ Consider using PBL as part of your teaching practice. ☐ Use PBL in your personal life when faced with unknown situations. ☐ Commit to using PBL fully so you aren't tempted to take shortcuts.
Here's How	

Think about PBL. How would you go about implementing it? Think about resources you can access to make this work for you. Are those resources human, print, online, or other? Take some time to read and learn more about PBL. As you become more comfortable with it, consider using it as a teaching method in your classroom and with your students. You might want to start with a PBL project. Work toward giving students more control over their learning. Remember to let your students struggle a bit, and don't just give them the answers. Talk with colleagues to design and use a PBL event. Share ideas about activities that allow your students to explore and learn on their own.

As you use PBL in your own practice, you will begin to see more opportunities for the method in your personal life. Make use of those! Help yourself to think through a small problem, using the categories on the PBL Learning Grid as a guide to thinking. If you don't already, keep a journal and reflect on your use of the method. Make notes in your journal regarding what you have learned and what you want to learn. Feel free to contact an expert in the field of PBL for advice on how to move to the next level.

PART II
PBL *training* modules

CHAPTER 4

Shifting From Teaching to Learning

What is the purpose of school? It seems like a simple question with an easy answer, yet far too many schools are missing their fundamental purpose: student learning. Teachers enter the profession because they are committed to the well-being of children and youth. It is a calling we take seriously. We primarily focus on student needs, but we sometimes shift our focus to ourselves and our practice, which is necessary. However, when the focus is on teaching instead of learning, many educators become comfortable with *providing opportunities* for students to learn rather than *ensuring learning* for all students. This is why implementing the PLC process requires a shift in attitude from teaching to learning. To make this shift, schools undertaking PLC transformation must understand the four pillars of a PLC.

This chapter will focus on these four pillars, provide the Think This, Do This framework to guide teams in transforming their thinking and action, and share a PBL module—the Fundamentals—to help teams transform from traditional schools to PLCs that focus on student learning rather than on teaching.

The Four Pillars

PLCs are built on four foundational pillars for student learning: mission, vision, values (collective commitments), and goals (DuFour et al., 2024). The mission statement of a school answers the question, "Why do we exist?" Answers to this question should foster a vision that asks, "What do we hope to become?" Many schools are content to create written documents with well-crafted mission and vision statements. Stopping there misses their true value. Educators must strive to align the mission and vision of the school to the values and goals that direct their work. This spurs a response to the question, "What commitments must we make to create the school or district that will improve our ability to fulfill our purpose?" followed by "What goals will we use to monitor our progress?" (DuFour, DuFour, & Eaker, 2008; DuFour et al., 2024).

Mission

Why may be one of the most asked questions of any teacher. Students constantly want to know why they are required to learn specific information. Educators crave answers to the same question. They want to know why they are expected to do certain things in a specified way. If a school can become clear on its purpose and mission statement, then teachers and students can be moved to focus on specific acts of improvement, which will be more impactful for student learning. Author Victoria Bernhardt (2018) explains the difference between random acts of improvement and focused acts of improvement. A school with focused acts of improvement has more success than a school with random acts because the focused acts are all centered on the same target. Bernhardt (2018) states, "A school defines its future through its mission, vision, goals, and student expectations" (p. 117). By answering the mission statement question of "Why do we exist?" the school is able to clarify its priorities and sharpen its focus on the target of learning for all students (DuFour et al., 2024).

The mission of learning for all students propels the work of the collaborative teams in a PLC. Writing the mission statement does not end the work; it *begins* the hard work that must occur to ensure alignment of the vision, values, goals, policies, and procedures within the school. As Richard DuFour, Rebecca DuFour, and Robert Eaker (2008) state, "If educational leaders are not prepared to be tight regarding the core purpose of their organizations, if they are not prepared to communicate that purpose clearly and consistently, if they are not prepared to insist that their schools and districts align their practices then they will not create PLCs, regardless of what else they are tight about" (p. 119).

Use the "Think This, Do This: The Purpose of School" reproducible tool (page 66) with collaborative teams to examine actions to take regarding the mission of your PLC.

Vision

In *The Vision-Driven Leader*, author Michael Hyatt (2020) provides specific instructions on how vision-driven leaders can inspire their teams. Hyatt tells the story of eleven-year-old Pakistani girl Malala Yousafzai, who asked the question, "How dare the Taliban take away my basic right to education?" She went on to become the youngest person to ever win a Nobel Peace Prize and has since begun an organization that is helping to educate girls across the world. Malala had a vision. Educators need to get a vision as well.

Hyatt asks a series of questions in his book to assist in creating a vision that drives leaders. First, one must answer the question of what you want. Until an answer to this question is clearly understood by all, action should not begin. Next, ask if what we want is clear. Is it concrete? Is it explicit? Does it inspire? Is it practical? Answers to these questions will assist in formulating a vision that everyone in the organization deeply desires to come to fruition. Clarity breeds confidence (Hyatt, 2020). Although educators will never be able to promise a perfect environment for learning to occur, "In times of uncertainty, clarity is the next best thing" (Stanley, 2020).

A school implementing its mission through an inspired vision of helping all children learn causes every employee of the school to recognize the importance of their work. Inspired educators will not allow any circumstance to deter them from the vision.

DuFour and colleagues (2008) present a three-question approach for evaluating the quality of a vision statement.

1. Does the vision result in people throughout the organization acting in new ways that are aligned with the intended direction that has been established?
2. Do people at all levels use the statement to guide their day-to-day decisions?
3. Is the statement used to modify structures, processes, and procedures to better align with the intended direction of the school or district? (pp. 142–143)

Use the "Think This, Do This: Practice, Policy, and Procedures" reproducible tool (page 67) with collaborative teams to examine actions to take regarding the vision of your PLC.

Values (Collective Commitments)

To realize the mission and vision of learning for all, educators must evaluate what values they are willing to promote and defend. The high-quality education we desire for our own children and those in our lives should be what we desire for the students within our sphere of influence. For all students to learn, every educator in the school must make collective commitments—how must we behave—to one another and then follow these commitments (DuFour et al., 2024). For mission and vision statements to become more than mere words on paper, they must drive the daily decision-making process (Kanold, 2011). Educators must answer the question, "What would observers see us doing?" (Senge, Kleiner, Roberts, Ross, & Smith, 1994, p. 302) because values are expressed through daily actions. The answers to this question—the collective commitments—should be written down and clearly described to make clear how teams will live these values (Blanchard, 2009).

Use the "Think This, Do This: Collective Commitments" reproducible tool (page 68) with collaborative teams to examine actions to take regarding the values of your PLC.

Goals

Once teams of teachers have a compelling sense of why, a sincere desire for all students to learn, and clarity in their collective commitments to one another and the students they serve, then they are prepared to write goals to properly measure their growth. Goal setting is a common activity, yet when individuals do not know their why, they often fail to produce effective goals (Doerr, 2017). As collaborative teams in a PLC connect with the collective why, they are more able to master their motivation to persevere.

The definition of a collaborative team explicitly states the interdependent work of the team members revolves around the achievement of a common goal (DuFour et al., 2024). The PLC at Work process describes a method for creating goals that align with the school's mission and vision: SMART goals that are strategic and specific, measurable, attainable, results oriented, and time bound (Conzemius & O'Neill, 2014; DuFour et al., 2024). These SMART goals provide direction, and, since the PLC at Work process is a journey and not a destination, they provide a method for marking progress along the way. When teacher teams collectively develop and assess their team SMART goals, they have opportunities to determine if their efforts are being successful and provide feedback, including both time and support, to help students achieve at high levels.

> **SMART Goals**
>
> **Strategic and specific:** Each goal is aligned with the mission and vision of the organization and is succinctly crafted to avoid ambiguity.
>
> **Measurable:** Each goal can be assessed to measure progress.
>
> **Attainable:** All members of the team believe in their collective ability to achieve each goal.
>
> **Results orientated:** The focal point of each goal is specific student learning rather than teacher-centered activities.
>
> **Time bound:** A timeframe for accomplishing the goal, and for specific actions to occur, is addressed in each goal (DuFour et al., 2024).

We include celebrating in the goal section because celebration requires access to evidence of growth, and SMART goals are measurable. Celebrations indicate what we value. Celebrating progress, even incremental progress, encourages teams and teachers to continue to persevere and reminds teams of the priorities and what it takes to achieve them. Given the "overwhelming evidence that hope spurs on achievement" (Kouzes & Posner, 1999, p. xx), schools are remiss to neglect to celebrate growth.

Use the "Think This, Do This: Goal Setting" reproducible tool (page 69) with collaborative teams to examine actions to take regarding the goals of your PLC.

Focus on the Fundamentals

Understanding the concepts and actions related to mission, vision, values, and goals in a PLC helps to create a solid foundation for PLC transformation (DuFour et al., 2024). However, it is not a stopping point. There remains much work to do. The remainder of this chapter provides a PBL event designed to address the creation of a mission for a fictional school. While the content is used to support the main points of this chapter, the format (a problem to be solved) demonstrates PBL's usefulness in helping collaborative teams develop a PBL mindset in which they function more effectively by identifying problems, analyzing them, discovering new relevant knowledge, and staying on course toward solutions. This chapter's PBL event—the Fundamentals—could be utilized as a tool both for learning how to use the PBL method and for understanding the need for collectively developing a school mission statement.

The Fundamentals
PBL Module Facilitator Notes

This section contains background information to assist the facilitator in understanding the context of the PBL event. The purpose of this problem-based learning event is to introduce participants to the concept of mission in a PLC. You will notice that the terms *PLC* and *professional learning community* are intentionally omitted from the PBL scenes. It is important to not allow previous interactions with PLC to skew participants' thinking about the fundamental concept of collectively building a mission for a school.

This PBL event can be conducted in a two-hour session. Read the following facilitator materials and scenes prior to beginning the session to have a complete understanding of the PBL event. Present the three scenes sequentially with discussion occurring at the close of each scene. Often, participants will pose questions after reading scene 1 that will be answered in scene 2 or 3. Recording those questions on the reproducible "PBL Learning Grid: The Fundamentals" (page 70) helps to reveal the learning from the scenes for the entire group.

Roles and Responsibilities

As the facilitator, your task is to manage the PBL process during the entire learning event. First, explain the group roles and how to use the PBL Learning Grid. Referring to the group roles and responsibilities in table 4.1, assign someone to serve as the manager and another person to serve as scribe. Give copies of individual scenes to the manager for each team if you are training multiple collaborative teams and explain that they will be leading the group discussion and should only read the scenes one at a time. Stress the importance of not rushing through the scenes. They should allow enough time for the group to fully think through the problem.

TABLE 4.1: *PBL Group Roles and Responsibilities*

Group Role	Responsibility
Facilitator (administrator, academic coach, or team leader)	Act as a guide to ensure that all teams and individuals are fully exploring the content.
Manager	Manage the PBL process. Read each scene aloud and moderate discussions.
Scribe	Take group notes using the PBL Learning Grid and distribute information to the group.
Researcher (every participant, including manager and scribe)	Contribute to group discussions, research assigned tasks, and present findings to the group.

*Visit **go.SolutionTree.com/PLCbooks** to download a free reproducible version of this table.*

Next, groups should move to scene 1 (page 71). The manager will read the scene with no personal interpretation, and the group will begin to analyze the problem using the "PBL Learning Grid: The Fundamentals" (page 70). Encourage participants to summarize key information first, and then move across the PBL Learning Grid, using it as a method of brainstorming. Make sure they are allowing enough time at the end of the session to generate learning tasks for each group member.

As the facilitator, you should take a hands-off approach as much as possible. Allow participants to struggle with concepts and direction. You may intervene with guiding questions that serve to nudge the group in the desired direction. This will most likely occur as the group answers the question, "What do we need to know?" Do not direct the problem-solving process but allow time for the group members to raise issues, discuss options, and talk about alternative solutions. Remember to keep the contents of the facilitator's portions of this guide to yourself—there are notes that are meant for your eyes only.

Introduction to the PBL Event

Fundamentals may not always be fun, but they are essential! In a school that uses the PLC at Work process, goals must align with the mission, vision, and values. These are fundamental building blocks for success. When all other actions of the school also align with this foundation, schools can witness academic success for their students. This PBL event begins a series of episodes with Benjamin Franklin Middle School as they begin their PLC journey.

Problem

In the PBL event, Carla Newberry is a veteran teacher at Benjamin Franklin Middle School. The scene begins with her arrival at the first day of teacher in service for the new school year. What makes this year different is that the former principal retired, so today she and her colleagues will meet the new principal, Kenneth Kindred. In the three scenes that make up the PBL event, Principal Kindred reveals his plan to have teachers work collaboratively to reflect on the school's mission and vision. The scenes reveal some of the staff members' apprehension about the changes. Participants will work through the event collaboratively to reveal their thought processes and the necessary actions to implement the fundamentals of a PLC in their school.

Learning Objectives

The learning objectives follow the format found in the revision of Bloom's taxonomy (Armstrong, 2010). The purpose of the taxonomy is to organize learning experiences in a progression from basic knowledge, through application of the knowledge, and arriving at more complex levels of understanding, such as analysis and creative efforts. PBL events allow participants the opportunity to create new products and solutions on their own. For the Fundamentals PBL event, participants will:

+ Identify the importance of collectively developing a school mission and in using it to guide the daily activities of the faculty. (Remember)
+ Compare their fundamental purpose with the existing school mission statement. (Understand)
+ Produce a list of the fundamental purpose for school. (Apply)
+ Reflect upon their experiences and evaluate their findings. (Analyze)

Products

The product for a PBL event is always tied to real-world applications. Such products will reflect the day-to-day practice of teaching professionals. The desired product for this PBL event reflects what happens when a team of professionals works together to create a mission statement for the school. The purpose is for the team to create a statement that is relevant to their practice that is a "living document" that can be revised based on changes in professional circumstances. Ultimately, this leads to an alignment of mission, vision, and values (collective commitments) and focuses attention on the team goals that members will use in day-to-day practice. For the Fundamentals PBL event, participants will:

+ Write the current school's mission statement from memory.
+ Meet in groups to compare the fundamental purpose of school with their own school's mission.
+ Produce a list of the fundamental purpose of school and create a list of actions they will commit to do to fulfill the stated mission.

Assessments

In problem-based learning, the facilitator can use assessments to assess the progress of the group, or participants can use assessments for self-evaluation. The primary goal is for participants to evaluate their own progress and apply what they have learned on an ongoing basis. For the Fundamentals PBL event:

+ The facilitator will observe and make mental note of individual and group understanding.
+ Individuals will self-assess their progress and openly express their commitment to these actions.

Table 4.2 illustrates the alignment between the PBL learning objectives, products, and assessment.

TABLE 4.2: *PBL Learning Objectives, Products, and Assessment Alignment*

Learning Objectives	Products	Assessment
(Remember) Participants will identify the importance of collectively developing a school mission and in using it to guide the daily activities of the faculty.	Individuals will write the current school's mission statement from memory.	Facilitator will observe and make mental note of individual and group understanding.
(Understand) Participants will compare their fundamental purpose with the existing school mission statement.	Individuals will meet in groups to compare the fundamental purpose of school with their own school's mission.	Facilitator will observe and make mental note of individual and group understanding.
(Apply) Participants will produce a list of the fundamental purpose for school.	Individuals will produce a list of the fundamental purpose of school.	Facilitator will observe and make mental note of individual and group understanding.
(Analyze) Participants will reflect upon their experiences and evaluate their findings.	Individuals will create a list of actions they will commit to do to reach the stated mission.	Individuals will self-assess their progress and openly express their commitment to these actions.

Guiding Questions

The guiding questions for each scene will help you guide participant learning. When the manager is presenting the scenes, encourage participants to work through the problem on their own, using the reproducible "PBL Learning Grid: The Fundamentals" (page 70). They may flounder; that is OK. Remember, the learning comes in doing the work. Allow the participants to struggle and find answers to their own questions.

If participants approach you for information, resist the urge to answer questions. Instead, present one of the following questions.

+ Why do you ask that question?
+ Where would you expect to find the answer to that?
+ How would you be sure that the information you find is accurate and complete?

See the reproducible "Guiding Questions for the Fundamentals" on page 74 for questions to use during scenes 1, 2, and 3.

Resources

Resources can take two forms, those generated by the facilitator and those the participants discover. In a professional development setting, the latter are more important than the former. The facilitator can provide a loose structure by giving participants access to well-selected resources. Understand that the more resources you provide as a facilitator, the narrower the field of exploration on the part of the participant. For this PBL event, the following resources are suggested as an appropriate starting point.

+ DuFour, R., DuFour, R., Eaker, R., Many, T., Mattos, M., & Muhammad, A. (2024). *Learning by doing: A handbook for Professional Learning Communities at Work* (4th ed.). Bloomington, IN: Solution Tree Press.
+ DuFour, R., DuFour, R., Eaker, R., Mattos, M., & Muhammed, A. (2021). *Revisiting Professional Learning Communities at Work: Proven insights for sustained, substantive school improvement* (2nd ed.). Bloomington, IN: Solution Tree Press.

Time and Schedule

Every PBL event requires its own schedule; some take more time than others. Table 4.3 is the suggested calendar for this PBL event. The time suggestions should not be construed as the only way to proceed with this event. As the facilitator, use your best judgment for how much time participants require for each activity.

TABLE 4.3: The Fundamentals Schedule

Time	Activity	Resources Needed
15 minutes	Read and discuss scene 1. Record comments on the PBL Learning Grid.	"The Fundamentals: Scene 1" reproducible (page 71) and "PBL Learning Grid: The Fundamentals" (page 70)
5 minutes	Ask participants to write their school's current mission statement from memory.	

15 minutes	Read and discuss scene 2. Record comments on the PBL Learning Grid.	"The Fundamentals: Scene 2" reproducible (page 72) and "PBL Learning Grid: The Fundamentals" (page 70)
10 minutes	Ask participants to individually make a list of the fundamental purpose of school. Then, allow groups to discuss their lists.	
15 minutes	Read and discuss scene 3. Record comments on the PBL Learning Grid.	"The Fundamentals: Scene 3" reproducible (page 73) and "PBL Learning Grid: The Fundamentals" (page 70)
15 minutes	Conduct a whole-group discussion of the fundamental purpose of school and compile a list participants agree on.	Sticky notes Markers Whiteboard or posters
15 minutes	In small groups, compare the list to the school's current mission statement. Highlight areas from the list that are reflected in the mission statement. Cross out words in the mission statement that seem to contradict the fundamental purpose.	School's current mission statement
5 minutes	Conduct a whole-group discussion on the previous activity. Determine if the current mission statement reflects the school's fundamental purpose or if it needs to be changed (slightly or significantly).	
20 minutes	*Option 1: Small Groups* Produce mission statements to reflect each group's changes as previously discussed. Allow groups to share their work with the whole group. Discuss and vote for the statement that best reflects the whole. *Option 2: Whole Group* If participants are struggling to match mission to purpose, facilitate a whole-group discussion. Allow everyone to brainstorm their main fundamental purpose from their previous list. Post individual responses on the whiteboard and group together with like responses. Place identifying headings on these groupings. Use these to steer the group to consensus around main ideas, which will culminate in the writing of a mission statement. Note: In schools where the existing mission statement is deemed appropriate by the group, individuals should work together to reflect on the action steps required to meet the mission and develop commitments for cementing the mission statement into daily practice.	Sticky notes Markers Whiteboard or posters
5 minutes	Personal reflection: Each participant should read the mission statement and write their own interpretation of it. Then, they should create a list of actions they will commit to do to reach the stated mission.	

THINK THIS, DO THIS
The Purpose of School

Think This	Do This
The purpose of school is for all students to learn at high levels.	☐ Acknowledge the need for every student to learn at high levels. ☐ Acknowledge that educators can influence the learning of all students. ☐ Align all practices, policies, and procedures with the need for all students to learn at high levels. ☐ Believe all students can learn rather than making excuses as to why some students cannot learn. ☐ Make the changes that need to happen to fulfill the purpose of learning for all rather than relying on external forces.
Here's How	

With your team, consider each student you serve. Ask yourself which students do *not* need to learn the essential knowledge and skills of your content. Are there any students who do not need to learn it?

After acknowledging that every student needs to learn the content, consider specific items within your sphere of influence for the students you serve. Examine the practices, policies, and procedures of your team to determine if any of them are impeding student learning.

Create a list of specific items that may be hindering specific students' learning rather than fostering learning. Act on the list by addressing each item.

THINK THIS, DO THIS
Practice, Policy, and Procedures

Think This	Do This
The practices, policies, and procedures of school should promote high levels of learning for all students.	☐ Examine each practice, policy, and procedure to find how each can best promote high levels of learning for all students. ☐ Make necessary changes to any practice, policy, or procedure that is not operating in the best interest of student learning. ☐ Focus on changes within the team's control rather than derailing conversations with things that are out of the team's control. ☐ Ensure student needs come first rather than allowing the comfort of adults in the building to trump the needs of students.

Here's How

Refer to the list of specific items that may be hindering rather than fostering learning that your team created in the "Think This, Do This: The Purpose of School" mission activity. Examine the items individually. Are some items influencing others?

Collectively work to determine how to change each item until it functions in the best interest of student learning. This process may take time on the part of each team member to study and research best practices. It may be uncomfortable for many. Team members should hold one another accountable to the agreed-on belief that the team will do what is best for the learning of each student.

THINK THIS, DO THIS
Collective Commitments

Think This	Do This
Educators must honor collective commitments to one another and the students they serve.	☐ Collectively create a list of commitments that align with the mission and vision of the school. ☐ Be accountable to uphold the commitments that the team collectively created. ☐ Commit to a "no excuses" attitude for honoring collective commitments.

Here's How

As a team, read the school's mission and vision statements. Create a list of if / then statements aligned to the mission and vision. For example, *if* we believe that all students should learn at high levels, *then* we must provide high-quality teaching to every student. *If* every student should have high-quality teaching, *then* a variety of strategies will be necessary to meet the needs of every student. Continue this process until you have a list of actionable details.

From this list, create a set of commitments that each team member will honor to provide for the specific needs of each student daily.

THINK THIS, DO THIS
Goal Setting

Think This	Do This
Using goal setting and monitoring effectively provide teams with direction, a method for assessing progress, and specific evidence of success.	☐ Assess the current reality of the students' abilities to accomplish the skills and concepts in the upcoming unit of study. ☐ Collectively create SMART goals for the upcoming unit that connect to the mission and vision of the school. ☐ Collectively create a method to measure each goal. ☐ Reflect individually on a habit that will assist you in achieving the goals. ☐ Individually set habit goals that will assist you in achieving the goals. ☐ Collectively establish dates to regularly measure the progress your team is making toward your goals. ☐ Celebrate achievement of or progress toward meeting your goals.

Here's How

Consider the current reality of the students your team teaches related to the mission and vision of the school.

Develop a SMART goal or goals for the upcoming unit of study. As a team, discuss how to measure the goal and when to assess students. Discuss specific habits that could help your team and students achieve the goal.

In subsequent meetings, discuss progress toward the goal by analyzing student results using the measurement tool (assessment) the group determined. Discuss your individual habit goals to determine incremental progress.

Take time to celebrate progress. Acknowledging progress and allowing individual teachers to discuss what they are doing well provides positive reinforcement and encouragement for the team to keep working toward the goal.

At the end of the unit, analyze SMART goal or goals and adjust future instructional work according to the results. Repeat the process by developing the next SMART goal or goals based on students' current reality, the school's mission and vision, and the next unit of study.

PBL Learning Grid: The Fundamentals

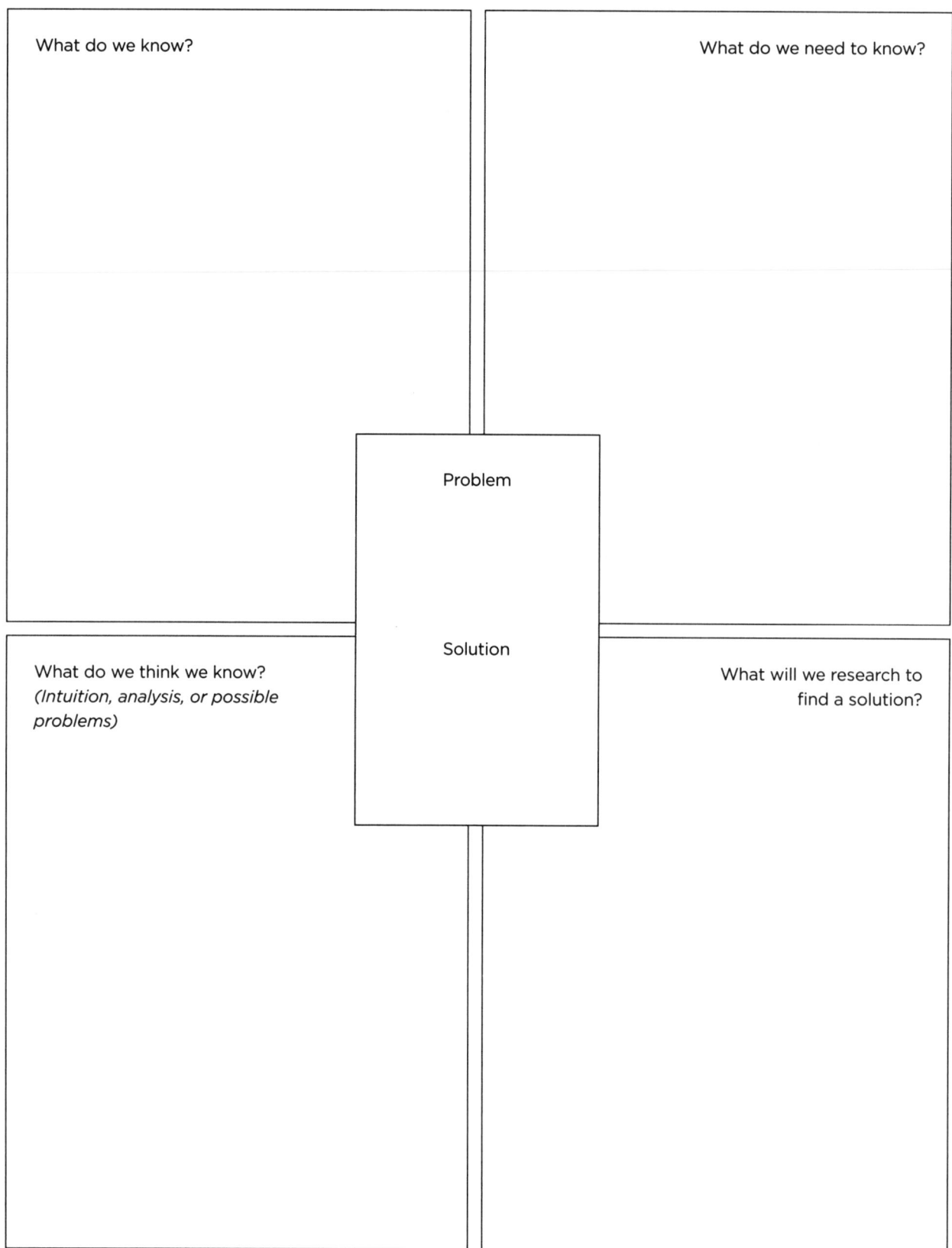

Mindset for Success © 2025 Solution Tree Press • SolutionTree.com
Visit **go.SolutionTree.com/PLCBooks** to download this free reproducible.

The Fundamentals: Scene 1

It was the start of another new school year, Carla Newberry's fifteenth at Benjamin Franklin Middle School. After all these years, she still looked forward to the first day of school as all the teachers met to prepare for the students' return. This year, however, there was a major difference: Principal Theo Morgan announced his retirement the previous spring. No one was really surprised; he had been in education for more than forty years. Principal Morgan was well respected and loved by all. To be honest, Carla most appreciated that he left everyone alone. She had the freedom to teach her sixth graders the required English curriculum without interference.

Carla enjoyed her students and the teachers on her grade-level hallway. The teachers had a tradition of gathering for a potluck on the last Friday of the month. If anyone had a birthday or special event, they always used this potluck to celebrate. It was good bonding time. Occasionally, someone on her hallway would mention an activity they did in their classroom. She loved it when she gained a new idea that she could use in her class. However, she did not know a lot about what went on in the other classrooms. This fact was of little concern to Carla because she felt confident in her abilities. Her students' scores on state assessments were in line with the average, so there was no need to worry. She often thought, "Well, I know I am doing better than *some* teachers, so they have to fire them first before they get to me."

Walking into the school's library on the first day, Carla felt good to be back in school. She was ready to tackle another school year, but also a bit nervous to meet her new principal. All would be fine, she thought. After all, there would be no need to make many changes; no reason to fix what is not broken.

As she entered the room, Carla sat her notebook and purse on the nearest open table and then walked to the line for refreshments. She waved at familiar faces and smiled at the few new faces she saw. Looking over the pastries, she overheard a conversation from two veteran teachers.

"What do you think 'mission and vision' means on the agenda?" asked Wanda Jones.

"I'm sure it is just a formality," said Marcus Lawson.

"Then why are there two hours devoted to it?" Wanda asked.

"That's weird. Surely he knows we already have a mission and vision statement," replied Marcus.

"Exactly! I need that time in my classroom to get ready to teach," Wanda snapped in exasperation.

Inwardly, Carla shared the same sentiment. She too needed to get her classroom ready for the school year. "But," she thought, "What is the mission statement for the school? I know it is painted on the front office wall, but has anyone ever read it?" After grabbing some fruit and a cup of coffee, Carla could not sit down until she had answered her own question. "What does the mission statement say?"

The Fundamentals: Scene 2

Within minutes of Kenneth Kindred introducing himself to the faculty, Carla knew that she liked him. His last name seemed to fit his personality well; the new principal was a kind man. She appreciated that he had taken a few minutes to introduce himself to the faculty before diving into the work of the school year. And she was impressed by the fact that he had moved his family into the school district upon taking this new job. Although his children were young, the fact that his twin boys would be old enough to come to Benjamin Franklin in the next couple of years spoke volumes about his commitment to the school.

When Principal Kindred moved to the next agenda item, he had transitioned so seamlessly that Carla did not recognize the switch. He explained the need for consistency and clarity among the faculty and staff. On each table, a stack of sticky notes had been provided along with markers. Principal Kindred asked each faculty member to take a pad and pen and create a list of the fundamental purpose of Benjamin Franklin Middle School. He asked each person to place only one idea per sticky note. After everyone had completed their own thoughts, each table was invited to share their lists with one another and craft a joint list for the table using the sticky notes. Everyone was given time to interact before Principal Kindred asked the tables to share their lists with the entire room. As they spoke, Mrs. Crystal Eastman, the new assistant principal, created a master list on the whiteboard. Once all the tables had shared their ideas, Principal Kindred asked everyone to review the list.

"Before beginning this school year, I want to have complete clarity on the purpose of our school," Principal Kindred stated. He then described a process for determining consensus. This "fist-to-five" method was meant to determine how much each person could support a decision. By scoring a five, participants were stating that they were ready to champion the decision. A four meant they strongly agreed with it. Three meant they thought it was okay and would go along. Two meant they had reservations and were not yet ready to support the decision. One indicated opposition. A fist meant the person wanted to veto the decision. Then, Principal Kindred asked the faculty to make their first decision of his administration. "If this was the agreed upon purpose of Benjamin Franklin Middle School, how much support could you show for it?"

Looking about the room, Carla was not surprised to see that most of the faculty voted a four or five. Even Wanda's two score was higher than she assumed it might be. Principal Kindred thanked the staff for their commitment to the school. "Before taking a short break, I would like to ask an important question," he stated. "Does the school's current mission statement reflect the fundamental purpose that we have just described?"

The Fundamentals: Scene 3

After the break, Assistant Principal Nancy Deal, the only remaining administrator from Principal Morgan's team, took the floor. She welcomed everyone back to another school year and shared a bit of her experience over the past two months with the faculty.

"I know change can be difficult," she stated, "but I am truly looking forward to watching Benjamin Franklin Middle School bloom. We have always been a great school, but I think we have the potential to be even better."

Carla noticed that all eyes were on Mrs. Deal while she spoke.

"Here is how we are going to begin," Mrs. Deal stated. "During the break, I placed a copy of the list that Assistant Principal Eastman was writing in our previous activity on each table. As a group, look at the current mission statement and see if the language reflects each item we stated in the previous list. Draw a line through any wording that is contrary to what we just stated was our fundamental purpose. Also, highlight any items that are not reflected in the mission statement."

As tables began working on the task at hand, Carla noticed that everyone at her table seemed to be enjoying this opportunity to plan for the upcoming year. It certainly was not what she expected when she entered the building a few hours earlier. She wondered if the people at Wanda's table were able to express their thoughts or if Wanda was monopolizing the conversation with mutterings of this being a waste of time. "I bet no one is having fun at that table," she thought to herself.

Guiding Questions for the Fundamentals

Scene 1

1. What do mission statements typically communicate?

2. What is the difference between a mission statement and a vision statement?

3. What is your experience with mission statements?

4. What do you think should be included in a mission statement?

5. If you had to characterize Benjamin Franklin Middle School, what would you say about it?

Scene 2

1. How would you identify an organization's values?

2. How would you identify an organization whose values are well reflected in its actions?

3. What does that look like?

4. What are some organizations that reflect their vision in their actions well?

5. How do schools compare to these other organizations?

6. With what you know now, how would you characterize Benjamin Franklin Middle School?

Scene 3

1. How do you ensure that the process of writing mission and vision statements is engaging, rewarding, and effective to everyone in the group?

2. With what you know now, how would you characterize Benjamin Franklin Middle School?

Final Reflection

1. Reflect on what you learned, not just about how to craft a mission statement, but on the process you used to identify the problem and how to solve it.

CHAPTER 5

Shifting From Isolation to Collaboration

St. Mark's Preschool in Murfreesboro, Tennessee, uses the story of *Stone Soup* to portray the importance of working together. *Stone Soup* is a classic folktale dating back to the 18th century. In the story, a poor, hungry man has an idea to get food from the local villagers. He takes an empty pot and fills it with water and a stone. Placing it over an open fire, he watches over the pot, stirring it from time to time. As villagers pass by, they each inquire as to what he is cooking. The poor man explains that he is making stone soup. With each approaching villager, he mentions that the soup needs a certain ingredient. One by one the villagers bring all the missing ingredients, and the story ends with everyone enjoying a bowl of delicious soup.

At St. Mark's Preschool, this tale takes on particular importance at an annual event near Thanksgiving. In preparation for the event, the children each bring an ingredient from home and help prepare the soup for all the families in attendance. It is a highlight of the year, and families enjoy the opportunity to watch their children interact with one another in such a positive way.

Though this lesson is taught at an early childhood level, the value of sharing and cooperation to complete a task has somehow been lost by many educators. Hardened by the pressures of the educational system, including heightened expectations coupled with stringent accountability measures, educators can easily forget what can be gained when they work together to solve a problem. For this reason, we are compelled to remind the reader of the fundamental value of working collaboratively and to explain how problem-based learning can help collaborative teams in a PLC transition from isolation to collaboration.

Within the PLC at Work literature, *collaboration* is defined as:

> A systematic process in which people work together, interdependently, to analyze and impact professional practice in order to improve individual and collective results. In a PLC, collaboration focuses on the critical questions of learning: What is it we want each student to learn? How will we know when each student has learned it? How will we respond when a student experiences difficulty in learning? How will we enrich and extend the learning for students who are proficient? (DuFour et al., 2008, p. 464)

The density of this definition makes it easy to overlook some important elements of collaboration and choose others that are more clearly understood. This leads to the formation of what we previously discussed as PLC Lite, in which teachers think they are doing the work of a PLC but are not gaining the full benefits of the PLC at Work process (DuFour et al., 2024). For this reason, we feel it is best to break the definition down into its components or parts for it to be more fully understood and appreciated.

The definition represents commitments in attitudes and actions, which must be made by each team member. These commitments include:

1. The systematic process itself,
2. Working interdependently with all team members, while,
3. Collectively working on specific items to improve individual and collective results.

A Systematic Process

The PLC at Work architects—Richard DuFour and Robert Eaker—were deliberate in selecting the term *systematic process* to begin the definition of collaboration. There are two aspects of the systematic process to consider. The first is to understand that PLC is not just a good idea, but a *process* that must be carried through in its entirety. To do so requires a commitment on the part of both teachers and administrators. Teachers must commit to using the PLC process to improve student learning. Likewise, thoughtful administrators must take the time to consider their responsibility in ensuring a systematic process is in place and supported so that collaboration occurs. For example, teachers do not create the master schedule—administrators do. Therefore, the responsibility is on the administrative team to carve out sufficient time for the teachers to collaborate with their team members. However, the mere act of allotting time does not complete the process. Rather, it is important to think of what happens during that slice of valuable time. Administrators often require teachers to work collaboratively on specific items or practices, yet the administrators themselves do not fully comprehend the actions required for each item. For this reason, it is imperative that administrative teams also work on these specific items to help their schools make significant gains. This is the true power of the phrase *learning by doing*, which the PLC architects have so thoughtfully employed.

Second, the systematic PLC at Work process is learned as teams do the work. They should not wait until they have a complete understanding of the work to begin doing it. Collaborative time will become systematic when it is framed and guided by specific actions. It is valuable to consider how the process meets the requirement of "framing and guiding." For that, we must turn to the remaining elements of the definition.

Use the "Think This, Do This: A Systemic Process" reproducible tool (page 86) with collaborative teams to examine actions to take regarding the process of collaboration in your PLC.

Working Interdependently

The definition expands on the concept of process by stating that collaboration is "a systematic process in which people work together, interdependently" (DuFour et al., 2008, p. 464). Highly collaborative teachers recognize the importance of working together, just as did the poor, hungry man from *Stone Soup*. This man understood that he was dependent on the local villagers, without whom he would die. Likewise, the villagers benefitted from working in tandem. A carrot, by itself, does not make soup, after all, and this is the truth of the folktale. By coming together, the entire community enjoyed a better meal than any one person would have had on their own. There is a valuable lesson here for any organization that wants to solve problems, of which schools are at the forefront. Whether the person bringing the stone or the one offering the carrot, each person's contribution has value and each ingredient, when taken together, helps to solve problems and reach overall goals. This is the true method, and worth, of interdependence.

The purpose of working interdependently is "to improve individual and collective results" for the students served. Although specific students may be randomly assigned to individual teachers, the collaborative team should collectively work for the good of all students, regardless of to whom they are assigned. Teaching is an ethical profession, composed of dedicated individuals who hold themselves to high standards. Clearly, such teachers will work for the good of all students, not just some. However, it is not enough to simply care for all or even to be committed to the mission of assisting every student to learn because it is no longer possible for one teacher to work in isolation and meet the needs of all students. The explosion of knowledge and the expansion of the application of that knowledge has left many well-meaning teachers struggling to keep up. More and more, it is apparent that teachers who work in isolation end up addressing the needs of some students more than others. As mentioned before, a commitment to the idea of collaboration is not enough. Further, collaboration depends on other commitments. The process may be carried out fully, but by itself, it will have little effect if teachers are not committed to focusing the process on the right work.

Use the "Think This, Do This: Working Interdependently" reproducible tool (page 87) with collaborative teams to examine actions to take regarding the process of collaboration in your PLC.

Working Collectively on Specific Items

In the *Stone Soup* folktale, each new person brought a specific item to add to the soup. One villager supplied vegetables, another provided meat, and a third furnished the seasonings. With each contribution, the stone soup improved and began to take on the flavors of each ingredient. The ingredients were not randomly selected, however. The villagers brought what they did because the "cook," or organizer of the project, had explained what the soup needed. In like manner, the PLC at Work process outlines the exact needs for the collaborative work of teams to make the cultural shifts in their collaborative work. The following list is specific, containing items that reflect a shift *from* one behavior *to* another.

- A shift from isolation to collaboration.
- A shift from each teacher clarifying what students must learn to collaborative teams building shared knowledge and understanding about essential learning.
- A shift from each teacher assigning priority to different learning standards to collaborative teams establishing the priority of respective learning standards.
- A shift from each teacher determining the pacing of the curriculum to collaborative teams of teachers agreeing on common pacing.
- A shift from individual teachers attempting to discover ways to improve results to collaborative teams of teachers helping each other improve.
- A shift from privatization of practice to open sharing of practice.
- A shift from decisions made based on individual preference to decisions made collectively by building shared knowledge of best practices.

- A shift from "collaboration lite" on various matters to collaboration explicitly focused on issues and questions that most impact student achievement.
- A shift from an assumption that these are "my kids, those are your kids" to an assumption that these are "our kids." (DuFour et al., 2008, p. 94)

Each of these items requires a shift in the way we think through situations and solve related problems. This shift may be thought of as a sensible approach to thinking and problem solving, and that "sensible thinking" process is the PBL mindset. In a cycle of continuous improvement, users of the PBL mindset recognize that individuals solve problems better when they work with others. PBL requires collaboration, and teachers who achieve a PBL mindset recognize the value of sharing thoughts and insights with one another. Herein is the profound relationship between PBL and PLC at Work: the commitment to sensible thinking inherent in PBL leads to the PBL mindset, which helps us to *think through a problem*. Likewise, the PLC at Work model also requires a firm commitment—to collaborative problem solving. This powerful combination of commitments ensures better outcomes as teams truly embrace the practice of working toward the goal of improved student learning. So, as with any shift in thinking, the mindset is the result of *practicing the method*.

Use the "Think This, Do This: Working Collectively on Specific Items" reproducible tool (page 88) with collaborative teams to examine actions to take regarding the process of collaboration in your PLC.

Focus on Collaboration

When real, effective collaboration takes place, it shows most powerfully in the practices that teachers use in their own work. Their effectiveness at establishing best practices is a result of how much they value collaboration and how well they implement the practice in their team meetings. Strict adherence to the shared goals of practice, specifically stated and planned for, using PBL, will lead collaborative teams to outcomes such as shared pacing, where teachers are moving in tandem through the shared experiences, and sharing ideas for improvement, where teachers reflect as a team on their effectiveness and make improvements in practice as they move along. The effect multiplies as teachers see the positive results in student learning. Success in purpose builds a sense of community as teachers become open about those ideas and even support each other in practice. Highly effective teachers share students and divide responsibilities, based on the needs of the learners. As the process gains strength, it becomes a part of the culture of the school and strengthens the belief that "these are our kids, not just my kids."

The remainder of this chapter provides a PBL event designed to introduce participants to the concept of collaboratively planning with the four PLC critical questions. While the content is used to support the main points of this chapter, the format (a problem to be solved) demonstrates PBL's usefulness in helping collaborative teams develop a PBL mindset in which they function more effectively by identifying problems, analyzing them, discovering new relevant knowledge, and staying on course toward solutions. This chapter's PBL event—the Writing on the Wall—could be utilized as a tool both for learning how to use the PBL method and for understanding the need for collectively understanding the need for collaboration.

The Writing on the Wall
PBL Module Facilitator Notes

This section contains background information to assist the facilitator in understanding the context of the PBL event. The purpose of this problem-based learning event is to introduce participants to the concept of collaborative planning with the four PLC critical questions. You will notice that the terms *PLC* and *professional learning community* are intentionally omitted from the PBL scenes. It is important to not allow previous interactions with PLC to skew participants' thinking about the fundamental concept of collaborative planning.

This PBL event can be conducted in a two-hour session. Read the following facilitator materials and scenes prior to beginning the session to have a complete understanding of the PBL event. Present the three scenes sequentially with discussion occurring at the close of each scene. Often, participants will pose questions after reading scene 1 that will be answered in scene 2 or 3. Recording those questions on the reproducible "PBL Learning Grid: The Writing on the Wall" (page 89) helps to reveal the learning from the scenes for the entire group.

Roles and Responsibilities

As the facilitator, your task is to manage the PBL process during the entire learning event. First, explain the group roles and how to use the PBL Learning Grid. Referring to the group roles and responsibilities in table 5.1, assign someone to serve as the manager and another person to serve as scribe. Give copies of individual scenes to the manager for each team if you are training multiple collaborative teams and explain that they will be leading the group discussion and should only read the scenes one at a time. Stress the importance of not rushing through the scenes. They should allow enough time for the group to fully think through the problem.

TABLE 5.1: PBL Group Roles and Responsibilities

Group Role	Responsibility
Facilitator (administrator, academic coach, or team leader)	Act as a guide to ensure that all teams and individuals are fully exploring the content.
Manager	Manage the PBL process. Read each scene aloud and moderate discussions.
Scribe	Take group notes using the PBL Learning Grid and distribute information to the group.
Researcher (every participant, including manager and scribe)	Contribute to group discussions, research assigned tasks, and present findings to the group.

*Visit **go.SolutionTree.com/PLCbooks** to download a free reproducible version of this table.*

Next, groups should move to scene 1. The manager will read the scene (see reproducible page 90; scenes 2 and 3 follow on pages 92–94) with no personal interpretation, and the group will begin to analyze the problem using the PBL Learning Grid. Encourage them to summarize key information first, and then to move across the PBL Learning Grid, using it as a method of brainstorming. Make sure they are allowing enough time at the end of the session to generate learning tasks for each group member.

Take a hands-off approach as much as possible. Allow participants to struggle with concepts and direction. You may intervene with guiding questions that serve to nudge the group in the desired direction. This will most likely occur as the group answers the question, "What do we need to know?" Do not direct the problem-solving process but allow time for the group members to raise issues, discuss options, and talk about alternative solutions. Remember to keep the contents of the facilitator's portions of this guide to yourself—there are notes that are meant for your eyes only.

Introduction to the PBL Event

Schools around the world have mission statements written on their walls, but few teachers working in the schools are moved to action by these words. At Benjamin Franklin Middle School, the writing on the walls is still fresh. The new mission statement has not just been painted on the wall; the actions of the professionals in the building have changed to match the fundamental purpose of the school.

Problem

At Benjamin Franklin Middle School, as Principal Kindred leads the faculty through the PLC process, many teachers are unsure of the right work they are supposed to be doing. They have not collaborated as teams in a PLC before; even though Carla has worked with her same-grade colleagues Michelle and Trent for many years, most of their work was done in isolation. As the team answers the first two critical questions of a PLC in three scenes, participants will reflect on their work with one another in collaborative teams and the progress of the fictional team, and consider how their work aligns with the mission of the school.

Learning Objectives

The learning objectives follow the format found in the revision of Bloom's taxonomy (Armstrong, 2010). The purpose of the taxonomy is to organize learning experiences in a progression from basic knowledge, through application of the knowledge, and arriving at more complex levels of understanding, such as analysis and creative efforts. PBL events allow participants the opportunity to create new products and solutions on their own. For the Writing on the Wall PBL event, participants will:

+ Identify the right work to accomplish during collaborative meetings. (Remember)
+ Compare a previous unit plan to the collaborative unit plan. (Understand)
+ Collaboratively produce a unit plan for an upcoming unit of study, including answers to the first two PLC critical questions—(1) What do we want students to know and be able to do? and (2) How will we know if they have learned it? (Apply)
+ Reflect on their experiences and evaluate their findings. (Analyze)

Products

The product for a PBL event is always tied to real-world applications. Such products will reflect the day-to-day practice of teaching professionals. The desired product for this PBL event reflects what happens when a team of professionals on a grade-level or content-specific team collaborates during planning with the four PLC critical questions. For the Writing on the Wall PBL event, participants will:

+ Create a list of activities they consider to be "the right work" of collaboration.
+ As a team, look back at a unit plan they previously used when they taught an upcoming unit. If no one in the group has taught the unit previously, they can brainstorm individually how they might teach it and then compare ideas.

+ As a team, create a unit plan and summative assessment for an upcoming essential standard.
+ Compare their answers to "What is the right work?" to the process they just experienced and then reflect on how these actions do (or do not) represent the list of actions they committed to do to reach the mission statement.

Assessments

In problem-based learning, the facilitator can use assessments to assess the progress of the group, or participants can use assessments for self-evaluation. The primary goal is for participants to evaluate their own progress and apply what they have learned on an ongoing basis. For the Writing on the Wall PBL event:

+ Facilitator will observe and make a mental note of individual and group understanding and support the process of learning as needed.
+ Participants will self-assess their progress and openly express their commitment to the right work.

Table 5.2 illustrates the alignment between the PBL learning objectives, products, and assessment.

TABLE 5.2: *PBL Learning Objectives, Products, and Assessment Alignment*

Learning Objectives	Products	Assessment
(Remember) Participants will identify the right work to accomplish during collaborative meetings.	Individuals will create a list of activities they consider to be the right work of collaboration.	Facilitator will observe and make a mental note of individuals' understanding.
(Understand) Participants will compare a previous unit plan to the collaborative unit plan.	Groups will look back at a unit plan they previously used when they taught an upcoming unit. If no one in the group has taught the unit previously, they can brainstorm individually how they might teach it and then compare ideas.	Facilitator will observe and make a mental note of individual and group understanding and support the process of learning as needed.
(Apply) Participants will collaboratively produce a unit plan for an upcoming unit of study, including answers to the first two PLC critical questions: (1) What do we want students to know and be able to do? and (2) How will we know if they have learned it?	Groups will create a unit plan and summative assessment for an upcoming essential standard.	Facilitator will observe and make a mental note of individual and group understanding and support the process of learning as needed.
(Analyze) Participants will reflect on their experiences and evaluate their findings.	Individuals will compare their answers to "What is the right work?" to the process they just experienced. They will then reflect on how these actions do (or do not) represent the list of actions they committed to do to reach the mission statement.	Individuals will self-assess their progress and will openly express their commitment to these actions.

Guiding Questions

The guiding questions for each scene will help you guide participant learning. When the manager is presenting the scenes, encourage participants to work through the problem on their own, using the reproducible "PBL Learning Grid: The Writing on the Wall" (page 89). They may flounder; that is OK. Remember, the learning comes in doing the work. Allow the participants to struggle and find answers to their own questions.

If participants approach you for information, resist the urge to answer questions. Instead, present one of the following questions.

+ Why do you ask that question?
+ Where would you expect to find the answer to that?
+ How would you be sure that the information you find is accurate and complete?

See the reproducible "Guiding Questions for the Writing on the Wall" on page 95 for questions to use during scenes 1, 2, and 3.

Resources

Resources can take two forms, those generated by the facilitator and those the participants discover. In a professional development setting, the latter are more important than the former. The facilitator can provide a loose structure by giving participants access to well-selected resources. Understand that the more resources you provide as a facilitator, the narrower the field of exploration on the part of the participant. For this PBL event, the following resources are suggested as an appropriate starting point.

+ DuFour, R., DuFour, R., Eaker, R., Many, T., Mattos, M., & Muhammad, A. (2024). *Learning by doing: A handbook for Professional Learning Communities at Work* (4th ed.). Bloomington, IN: Solution Tree Press.
+ DuFour, R., DuFour, R., Eaker, R., Mattos, M., & Muhammed, A. (2021). *Revisiting Professional Learning Communities at Work: Proven insights for sustained, substantive school improvement* (2nd ed.). Bloomington, IN: Solution Tree Press.

Time and Schedule

Every PBL event requires its own schedule; some take more time than others. Table 5.3 is the suggested calendar for this PBL event. The time suggestions should not be construed as the only way to proceed with this event. As the facilitator, use your best judgment for how much time participants require for each activity.

TABLE 5.3: *The Writing on the Wall Schedule*

Time	Activity	Resources Needed
15 minutes	Read and discuss scene 1. Record comments on the PBL Learning Grid.	"The Writing on the Wall: Scene 1" (page 90) and "PBL Learning Grid: The Writing on the Wall" (page 89)
5 minutes	Individuals will write a list of their response to the question, "What is the right work?"	
15 minutes	Read and discuss scene 2. Record comments on the PBL Learning Grid.	"The Writing on the Wall: Scene 2" (page 92) and "PBL Learning Grid: The Writing on the Wall" (page 89)
10 minutes	The group will have preselected an upcoming essential standard. Individually, they will write what they think the standard is asking and how mastery could be determined. Then, individuals will share their interpretation with their team members and discuss similarities and differences.	Upcoming essential standard
15 minutes	Read and discuss scene 3. Record comments on the PBL Learning Grid.	"The Writing on the Wall: Scene 3" (page 94) and "PBL Learning Grid: The Writing on the Wall" (page 89)
15 minutes	Team members should discuss how the essential standard was assessed in the previous year. If they have access to last year's data, it should be made available. Discuss the mastery level of last year's students on the standard.	
40 minutes	Create a unit plan for the upcoming standard. Discuss prerequisite knowledge necessary to begin the unit as well as extension activities for students who have already mastered the content. Create an end-of-unit summative assessment that the team collectively agrees to use to assess student progress. Determine a date to analyze the results of the assessment.	
5 minutes	Personal reflection: Individuals compare their answers to "What is the right work?" to the process they just experienced. They will then reflect on how these actions do (or do not) represent the list of actions they committed to do to reach the mission statement.	

THINK THIS, DO THIS
A Systematic Process

Think This	Do This
A systematic process reaches its full potential when it is followed with fidelity.	☐ Read all information about a specific PLC task, process, or practice. ☐ Discuss the task, process, or practice with each member of your team until the team develops a common understanding. ☐ Follow a task, process, or practice with fidelity rather than picking and choosing portions to do or not do.

Here's How

Collaborative teams in a PLC learn how to work together by doing the work. Just as students develop at different rates, teams also develop their capacity to work collaboratively at differing times.

With your team, discuss an area of the PLC process that conflicts with how your team members have previously worked. Commit to one another to approach the topic with an open mind and try a different way.

Discuss the specifics of the PLC systematic process you will try. This may involve team members reading a portion of a PLC book (such as *Learning by Doing*; DuFour et al., 2024) or article from the *AllThingsPLC* Magazine or website (allthingsPLC.info).

Agree to try the process for a three-week period. At the end of that time, discuss the results with your team. Use the PBL Learning Grid (page 49) to guide your discussion. As you list what your team needs to know about the topic, discuss where you can go to find the information. Perhaps another team is excelling at this task and can help, or a member of the administrative team may have insight into where to find information. Agree to continue learning about this topic for another three-week period and repeat the debrief process.

Reference

DuFour, R., DuFour, R., Eaker, R., Many, T., Mattos, M., & Muhammad, A. (2024). *Learning by doing: A handbook for Professional Learning Communities at Work* (4th ed.). Bloomington, IN: Solution Tree Press.

THINK THIS, DO THIS
Working Interdependently

Think This	Do This
Working interdependently with my colleagues has the potential to help more students learn at a deeper level.	☐ Create a team goal that requires team members to need one another to accomplish the goal. ☐ Develop an action plan for accomplishing the goal. ☐ Make collaboration a requirement rather than allowing one or more team members to opt out of the collaborative process.

Here's How

Assess the current reality of the students your collaborative team serves. Look for a specific area of growth that students need as a whole or that individual groups of students require.

Develop a SMART goal to address the area of need. Establish specific actions for team members to complete. Create a corresponding timeline to measure progress toward the SMART goal.

At the next meeting, discuss the outcomes of the action steps to determine if the team should continue or discontinue these steps.

Mindset for Success © 2025 Solution Tree Press • SolutionTree.com
Visit **go.SolutionTree.com/PLCBooks** to download this free reproducible.

THINK THIS, DO THIS
Working Collectively on Specific Items

Think This	Do This
There are specific concepts that every student must understand for every subject taught in schools.	☐ Work collectively with your grade-level or content-specific team to come to a consensus on the meaning and intention of the standards you are required to teach. ☐ Work collectively with these same teachers to determine a list of specific skills and concepts that are essential for every student to understand. ☐ Work collectively to develop a common method of assessing each skill and concept. ☐ Choose only skills and concepts that are essential rather than attempting to make every national, state, provincial, or district standard essential. ☐ Work collaboratively through the entire process rather than dividing up the work for individual teachers to do part while other teachers do other parts.

Here's How

Work collaboratively to choose an upcoming unit of study. Read the national, state, provincial, or district standards the unit of study addresses. Discuss the individual standards to determine if each teacher is interpreting the standard in the same way.

If multiple interpretations exist, use available resources to decide on one meaning of the standard. These resources may differ per location.

Next, come to consensus about the essential skills and concepts that must be taught in this unit. Make a list of each essential skill and concept.

Collectively develop a method to assess each essential skill or concept on the list. If necessary, develop a rubric or checklist that each teacher will use to assess the skill or concept.

The purpose of this activity is not just to get the work done. The purpose is to develop a deep understanding of the topics being taught and to ensure that each teacher interprets them the same way. Therefore, it is essential to do this work collectively, rather than to simply divide and conquer the work.

PBL Learning Grid: The Writing on the Wall

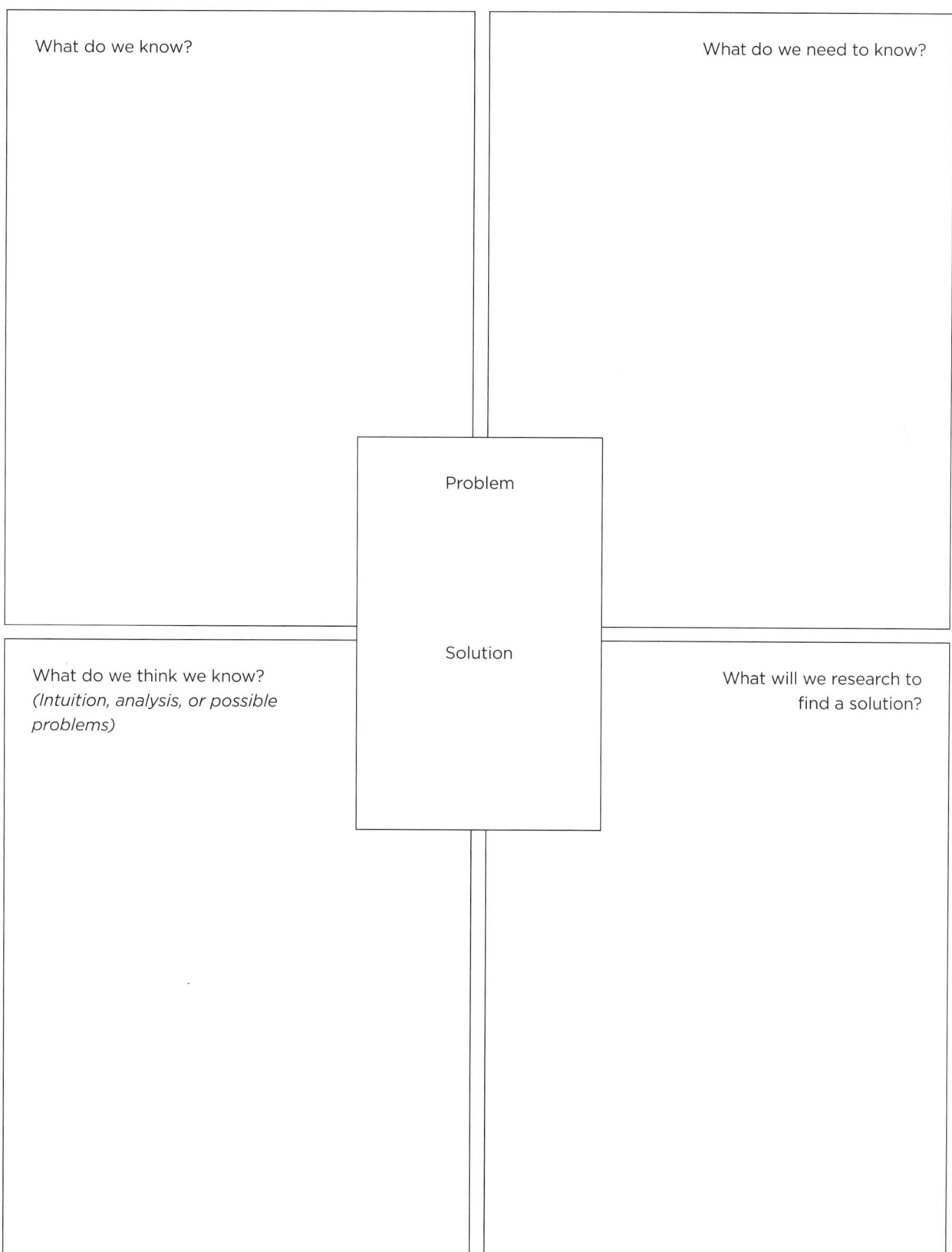

| What do we know? | What do we need to know? |

Problem

Solution

| What do we think we know? *(Intuition, analysis, or possible problems)* | What will we research to find a solution? |

Mindset for Success © 2025 Solution Tree Press • SolutionTree.com
Visit **go.SolutionTree.com/PLCBooks** to download this free reproducible.

The Writing on the Wall: Scene 1

The atmosphere in Principal Kindred's conference room was very pleasant as Carla met with the other members of the leadership committee. Behind Principal Kindred, a newly printed sign hung on the wall with the new school mission statement: "Learning for all." Not only was Carla happy to admit that she now knew what the mission statement said, she was excited about the words. Learning for all, *period*. This is why Benjamin Franklin Middle School exists. This is why she works so hard every day as a teacher. She truly wanted every single student to learn. How to do that, however, was a different story.

"How are your collaborative meetings going?" was the question group members were discussing. Marcus Lawson, the mathematics department head, spoke first.

"It is different for some of the teachers in our building because they have never been asked to work collaboratively," he stated.

As he spoke, heads nodded in agreement. Principal Kindred prompted the team for more specific details. Ann Goodwin, the science department head, responded, "Well, um, I have one team member who is asking if she can be exempted from the meetings because *she does not need to collaborate*." Everyone in the room knew she was describing Wanda Jones, who never held back her negative opinions.

"Talk to me about the team norms that you collectively developed. Are you making sure to enforce those norms when you meet? Without a plan for addressing broken norms, then you really do not have norms," stated Principal Kindred. After a bit of discussion on appropriate ways to enforce the norms, the conversation shifted.

"Collaboration is meaningless if you are not collaborating on the right information," Principal Kindred added. "I am counting on each of you, as the department heads of this school, to help me convey this message to all the staff members. Just as the teachers are critically important to the success of our students' learning, you are critically important to the collaborative culture we are building."

Carla spoke first as Principal Kindred paused. "The research you have shown us regarding the need to collaborate instead of working in isolation has been very compelling. Personally, I am in favor of building a collaborative culture. My problem is that I do not know for sure what the right work is yet. I am not sure what we should be collaborating on, and fear I will lead my team astray."

"I am nervous too," stated Rick Norris, the social studies department head. "The idea of using data is great, but we have never shared data before. We really do not even know how to share data."

Mrs. Goodwin added, "I don't even know where to find the data. Are we talking about state assessment data or county benchmarks?"

Sensing the uneasiness in the room, Principal Kindred responded, "Well, yes, but what other sources of data do you have?" The room went silent.

Principal Kindred assured each member of the guiding coalition, "You are not in this alone. If this ship sinks, I am going down with you. When we say, 'Learning for all,' that includes each one of us. We are all trying to learn how to meet the needs of each student, kid by kid and skill by skill. This is not an easy task." A sense of relief filled the room. "What we need to do right now," Principal Kindred continued, "is to be clear on what is expected in the meetings and how we are going to report it. There are a lot of templates that we can use, or we can develop our own. All that really matters is that we are using the four critical questions to drive the work of our meetings."

Walking to the whiteboard on the side of the room, Principal Kindred picked up a marker and said, "So, where should we begin?"

The Writing on the Wall: Scene 2

Today's meeting was important. Carla had completely bought into the plans Principal Kindred had discussed in the first weeks of school; what she did not know was how seriously her teammates would take it. Trent Law and Michelle Thomas were great people. She had worked beside them on the sixth-grade hallway for the past five years, but she had never really worked *with* them, even though they all taught the same subject. Now, she was expected to lead the charge of changing the culture from isolation to collaboration. Entering Trent's room, she was nervous but also resolved to do her best to lead the team.

"Michelle, Trent, you two know me. I hope you know that I am not trying to change you or anything about what you do in your classrooms. I hope you know that my intentions are good," Carla began.

"Absolutely. I know you were not campaigning for more work to do," stated Michelle.

"I certainly did not want another task to take on. I am happy to see you as the department chair this year," affirmed Trent. "Principal Kindred has come with a leadership agenda. So far, I like what I am seeing. I think we can trust him," he continued. Both Carla and Michelle nodded in agreement. "I think so too," said Michelle.

"I am glad you feel that way," continued Carla. "I feel really good about the work we have already done. Principal Kindred has all of the department chairs reading about different items. I am excited for the chance to collaborate with you. That being said, I want to do it right."

"Me too," said Trent. "I am too competitive by nature to do this thing halfway. If I start something, I don't want to do it half-heartedly. So, where do we begin?"

"We are going to be taking minutes on a shared document throughout the year. We all have access to it on the shared drive, and the administration will be looking at it as well. We have access to everyone's documents if we want to look. There's nothing secret about it," Carla explained.

"Since Trent volunteered the use of his room and Carla is the department chair, would you like for me to act as the recorder and keep up the minutes?" Michelle asked.

"I make a motion to accept Michelle's offer," Trent teased. "Second the motion," replied Carla. "Motion passed," Trent replied with a laugh.

Carla loved the positive exchange between the three teachers, but she did not want it to get out of hand. She decided to pull up the document and begin looking at the work before them. "The question we must determine first is, What do we want our students to know and be able to do?" Carla stated.

"That is an easy question! They need to learn all the standards. Now, can we get a motion to adjourn?" Trent asked. "Sorry, Trent," replied Carla. "It's not that easy. We need to become students of the standards."

"What does that mean?" Michelle asked. After a lengthy discussion and looking at the state standards, the team narrowed their discussion to the upcoming unit of study. "We need to make sure we are all in agreement about what this standard is really asking, and then we need to answer the next critical question, How will we know if the students have learned it?" Carla explained.

A noise in the back of the room caught their attention. Mrs. Deal, their much beloved assistant principal, was sitting at a student desk. "Hello, Mrs. Deal, we did not even notice you were back there," Trent said.

"Sorry to scare you," she said. "I just want to sit in on some of the meetings since they are new this year. You guys are really doing a great job. Thinking about this second question makes me wonder something. Have you considered looking at the data on how the students did last year on this standard?"

The Writing on the Wall: Scene 3

"Last year's data—well, that's a novel idea," Trent replied.

"Can we take ten minutes to go pull out our materials from last year and then come back to the room?" Michelle asked.

"Yes, I think that is a great idea," said Carla. The three dispersed to their own classrooms with focused attention. *Last year's data*, Carla thought to herself. "What did I do last year for this standard?" she asked herself aloud as she looked through her filing cabinet. Finding her file of assessments for the year, she went to the front of the file. She always had a habit of placing one copy of her classroom tests in sequential order from the beginning of the school year to the last grading period. "I wish I remembered how the kids scored on this test last year. But I really don't recall," she thought.

Meeting back as a group, the team decided to read each person's assessment first. Carla began with Trent's assessment. She noticed several similarities to her own, where many questions were essentially the same as she had written. "I really like how he worded question three," she thought. "The format for question five is much better than what I used."

Looking at Michelle's assessment, she realized something important. Michelle had gone deeper into the content of the standard than either she or Trent had done. Her assessment allowed for more application of the standard whereas she and Trent had done more to simply repeat the facts.

"I have something to say!" Trent's voice broke the silence in the room. "Why have I been doing this work alone in my own room all these years? You two are rock stars! I am over here reinventing the wheel all by myself when I could have been building a better wheel with the two of you!"

"I couldn't agree more," Michelle stated. "I am excited about this process."

"Now, do you see what I mean about becoming a student of the standard?" Carla asked.

"Oh yes, I think I was doing too much," Michelle said. "Not me," Trent replied. "Seeing your test made me realize I did not go deep enough." The three began discussing the individual parts on each of their assessments.

"This is why the critical questions are so important," Carla began. "We have to make sure we are agreeing on what we want the students to know and be able to do. Without that, we cannot know how to commonly assess our students. Until we get that figured out, we will never be able to move on to the last two questions."

"If we are going to be doing this much deep thinking, then I will be sure to have caffeine in my room when we meet!" said Trent. "I am also going to get my steel-toed boots on before you ladies come back. No need to get my feelings hurt just because you two are better teachers than I am."

"What are you talking about, Trent? You were teacher of the year two years ago," Michelle reminded him.

"That's the great thing about building a collaborative culture," Carla proclaimed. "We all will grow as teachers, and, best of all, the students will benefit from our labors."

"I suppose we need to get on with the meeting then," Trent said. "How will we know that the students have learned it? What would evidence look like for this standard?"

Guiding Questions for the Writing on the Wall

Scene 1

1. What happens when a teacher does not want to contribute to the team?

2. How can we encourage others to work together to address our challenges?

3. How do you define *data*?

4. What are some of the ways that data are used to support teaching?

5. How do you define *good data*?

6. How do you feel about using data to inform your practice?

7. How do you recognize data that will inform you in your practice?

Scene 2

1. How does the transformation to a PLC cause Carla, Michelle, and Trent's relationship to shift?

2. Describe the important elements of this initial PLC meeting. As a follow-up, ask, "Why do you think that is important?"

3. How do you think Carla feels with her new role in the group?

4. What does it mean to be a student of the standard?

Scene 3

1. How does a teacher know what is most important to emphasize in a unit plan?

2. What is the role of data in preparing a unit?

3. What is the relationship between last year's data and this year's students?

4. How are we to be sure our teaching is supported by our data?

5. Why do you think these teachers looked at each other's assessment information?

Final Reflection

1. Reflect on what you learned, not just about how to work interdependently, but on the process you used to identify the problem and how to solve it.

CHAPTER 6

Shifting From Intentions to Results

You may have heard the saying, "Hope is not a strategy." While it is true that hope alone is not a strategic method to reach a result, the absence of hope can affect a person's psyche to the point of causing defeat. Let's consider the meaning of *hope*. A person with hope has a desire to see an expected outcome. It is not a simple wish but rather an expectation that the outcome is attainable. However, hope can't be realized in the absence of actions. This chapter addresses the need for appropriate actions toward the goal of student achievement *for all* in a PLC at Work.

The third big idea of a PLC is a focus on results (DuFour et al., 2024), where hope turns into action. In our experience, of the three big ideas of a PLC, this can be the most difficult to implement. Focusing on results rather than intentions can get personal for teachers—they may think blame for failure is being placed on them. However, analyzing results, especially those that don't reflect intentions, help teams answer the question of what students are not learning and why.

Shifting from intentions to results is at the heart of the PLC process and PBL. In problem-based learning, the point is to identify problems, describe them, categorize the knowledge and information needed to determine a workable solution, and take action to solve the problem. For example, a group of teachers may identify gaps in their students' learning. They would then devise methods to address these gaps, an assessment for measuring the results of these methods, and then modify their practice based on the results they measure. By doing something intentionally, they are marrying their intentions to actions for the purpose of producing results. When their intentions do not result in the desired effect, they use the new data to further identify the problem as they continue their search for an appropriate solution.

Imagine a group of seventh-grade social studies teachers as they consider the learning needs of their students. After administering a common assessment, the group decides to create a PBL Learning Grid. One teacher asks, "What do we know?" Another teacher laments, "The students are struggling with their map reading skills." This prompts the question, "What do we need to know?" to which another teacher states, "How can we make map reading relevant to twelve-year-old students?" As the teachers consider opportunities to make map reading relevant, they generate a list of items to research. The team decides to research orienteering, geocaching, and *Pokémon Go*.

When the team meets again later in the week, they discuss their findings and decide to create an outside activity to allow students to interact with a map and a compass to find "treasures" hidden around the campus. As the students interact in the activity, the teachers will complete a checklist of skills to determine if students are using the basic map elements. This will produce another set of data that the team can discuss in their subsequent meeting.

Use the "Think This, Do This: Turning Intentions Into Actions" reproducible tool (page 109) with collaborative teams to examine how good intentions must lead to actions in collaborative teams.

Making Decisions Using Data

Measuring results requires data. For many educators, the word *data* is akin to a curse word; yes, it is in fact a four-letter word, but that does not make it inherently bad. Schools are full of data. Thomas J. Peters and Robert H. Waterman (1982) state that schools suffer from the DRIP problem; they are data rich and information poor. Used correctly, data have the potential to become information. When teachers take the data they have and begin to think about it and compare it to other data points, then the data become information. Connecting information to other information to find associations between them transforms the information into knowledge. With knowledge, decision making is informed. Using this knowledge to create a clear path for decision making brings about wisdom.

Take for example the group of seventh-grade social studies teachers from earlier in the chapter. Upon completion of the "treasure hunt" activity, the teachers saw a common trend in the checklist data. Students were not orienting their maps before moving to the next destination on the map. This caused them to recognize the fact that most students never looked at the compass on the maps in the classroom. The students assumed that the top of the map represented the direction of north. The information from the checklist became knowledge when it was combined with additional information based on student observations. Here, we see how knowledge supported the team in making a wise decision for future classroom learning. The teachers would make a point to stress the importance of noticing the direction of the compass before answering map questions on the next assessment.

Teaching involves constant decision making. Sometimes, we hesitate to carry over what we do in our daily practice into the rest of our professional lives. There is a certain amount of risk involved. Decision making can be one of the scariest parts of any job because it requires us to make judgment calls in high-stakes situations, where we may be uncomfortable with the risks involved. Risk, no matter how great, can be addressed with preparation. Daniel Kahneman (2011) refers to the importance of not moving too quickly when a decision is required because of the interplay among three factors: "Jumping to conclusions is risky when the situation is unfamiliar, the stakes are high, and there is no time to collect more information" (p. 79). The lack of information, combined with high-stakes and unfamiliar circumstances, can have devastating and long-lasting effects on decisions made by teachers and school leaders alike. Urgency is the reality of daily life in schools, which points out the critical importance of data-based decision making in schools and in collaborative teams (Bernhardt, 2018; Reeves & Eaker, 2019).

In a PLC, results of teachers' decisions can be evaluated within a relatively small window of time. This evaluation provides further data to assist the teacher team with more mature and well-reasoned decisions regarding moving forward with individual student learning. The cycle of work within collaborative teams in a PLC allows teacher teams the ability to try new approaches and test their results in small segments of time throughout the school year. Rarely are decisions easy to make, especially educational decisions. However, using data to inform decision making should not frighten teachers if they work to have a better understanding of how to turn intentions into actions.

Using Data to Inform

Every school has a data profile that tells the story of the school (Bernhardt, 2018). This story is not written in stone, however. It can be changed—you "just have to know what it is. If you are not looking at all your data, you do not know the whole story of your school" (Bernhardt, 2018, p. 33). Educators often do not fully understand how to use their data to inform decisions. Bernhardt's (2018) work focuses on the decision path to move data from simply reporting the data to analyzing it, then using it to inform action, which then gives it value. Taken alone, numbers are just numbers; they do not have any real value until they are compared to other numbers. While this book does not explore the data-analysis process described in Bernhardt's book, individual teams can utilize the main points.

When teacher teams understand the power of using data to inform decisions, they will begin to shift their thinking about data use "from simple compliance to a true commitment to improvement" (Bernhardt, 2018, p. 2). With help, teachers can grow comfortable in comparing their data to other teachers' data. By understanding how they, as individual teachers, fit within the collective school system, they can understand why sharing data is integral to the success of all students.

Decision Making Within the System

Schools are learning organizations with individual parts that function in conjunction with other individual parts. All individuals within the learning organization are learners (Senge, 1990). A teacher makes up one individual part of the school system. While this teacher is a learner, he or she does not learn in isolation. The learning happens with the students and with the teachers in the building and school system. A team of teachers is thus learning to learn together. It should be said that it's okay to have failures in the PBL method. That is a way for us to grow and practice sensible thinking. This, then, is an opportunity for us to "learn about learning."

Additionally, each teacher makes decisions that affect others. As a member of the collective school system, interrelated actions of individual teachers can produce results with effects that take years to fully play out (Senge, 1990). For this reason, it is imperative for individual teachers to avoid focusing upon "snapshots of isolated parts of the system" (Senge, 1990, p. 7) as they ponder why the same problems persist. Finding solutions to the problems students face can only occur when teachers work collaboratively as they look across the system to find solutions.

Teachers working in a collaborative environment are positioned to avoid some of the pitfalls that cause systems to fail. Peter Senge (1990) describes different "learning disabilities" that cause the demise of organizations. These actions have the potential to be equally destructive in schools; however, when schools fail, it is the students who are adversely affected. For example, consider a task every teacher performs—grading student work. When the task of grading is viewed outside of its purpose of measuring student growth, teachers can easily mistake their own responsibility in this process of student learning. By viewing grading as a separate entity rather than a part of the learning system, teachers "have little sense of responsibility for the results produced when all positions interact" (Senge, 1990, p. 19).

A student's grade on a given topic provides a data point of their learning. To simply record the grade and move on to the next topic misses the point of the assessment. If the teacher wasn't going to use the data to inform the next actions, then why give the assessment? When a patient has a yearly physical examination, the doctor prepares a "grade sheet" of information gained from the blood test. This sheet is not simply filed away into the patient's records; rather it is discussed, and a plan of action is devised based on the results. For instance, if the results show that the patient's cholesterol level is high, the doctor might prescribe a certain meal plan for the patient to eat. The same thought process should guide teachers as they grade individual assessments. Rather than simply doing the daily tasks of the profession, educators need to recall the real purpose of the tasks they perform. This will help teachers to avoid another of the "learning disabilities" described by Senge (1990).

Each of us has the "propensity to find someone or something outside ourselves to blame when things go wrong" (Senge, 1990, p. 19). By viewing our actions in isolation, rather than viewing them as part of the whole, we cannot see how our own actions could play a part in the student's failure. Many times, excuses are made as to why a student scored poorly on an assessment. The student might be blamed for not paying attention or for not preparing for the assessment. If the assessment was created by an outside source, then it becomes easy to blame the problem on the assessment. While many of these excuses could be valid, the need for making excuses regarding students' performance on assessments needs to be removed. The assessment provides data about the student's current status along the learning progression of a given topic. When a team of teachers uses the graded work of a common formative assessment to discuss the data, they can begin to leverage the data to inform solutions to problems they jointly face. This allows teams to formulate a plan of action to help students move to the next level of learning.

Teams, in all types of organizations, often operate within self-protective norms that cause the individual members to become "proficient at keeping themselves from learning" (Senge, 1990, p. 21). Let's stop and ponder this statement for a moment. Is it possible that teachers have become "proficient at keeping themselves from learning"? The statement feels condescending and offensive. Now that we have acknowledged that fact, let's lay the emotions aside and try to understand the meaning behind the comment. Senge explains that a common mistake occurs when individuals rely heavily upon their own experience. Even though an individual may seemingly possess a large quantity of experience, it is still limited. Senge (1990) refers to this as a "learning horizon, a breadth of vision in time and space within which we assess our effectiveness" (p. 20). Since an individual's actions have consequences beyond their learning horizon, "it becomes impossible to learn from direct experience" because "we never directly experience the consequences of many of our most important decisions" (Senge, 1990, p. 20). This is also why it is so important to learn as a group with your teaching team.

Let's consider this within the context of grading student work. For each assessment, an overall grade can easily be scored and recorded. By stopping here, the teacher is not really learning anything from the assessment. However, if the assessment is analyzed based on each skill tested, then the teacher can begin to uncover which skills were best understood by the students. By analyzing the assessment skill by skill and student by student, the teacher can learn from the assessment. When these data are then shared with the other teachers on the team, additional information may be exposed. The team may discover trends across or within the individual teachers' classrooms. With this knowledge, the team is better prepared to decide upon the next course of action for the students.

Regrettably, when the common mistakes Senge (1990) describes are prominent among teachers, then decision making is often ill informed, causing our "proactiveness [to be] reactiveness in disguise" (p. 19). By not focusing on the system as a whole, teachers are unable to fully process how to make effective changes. Additionally, teachers become distracted from seeing long-term patterns because their focus is on isolated events. Rather, learning is a slow and gradual process requiring individuals to pause and reflect on both the subtle and dramatic (Senge, 1990). This requires time, a commodity that teachers all agree is insufficient.

Acting With Intention: Unit by Unit

When teams of teachers meet to discuss an upcoming unit of instruction, they can merge the four PLC critical questions with PBL. The first PLC critical question is, "What do we want the students to know and be able to do?" (DuFour et al., 2024). As team members answer this question, they can use the PBL Learning Grid to organize their thoughts. They might begin by asking, "What do we know about the essential standards for this unit?" and recording their answers on the grid. Further discussions may lead the team to ask, "What do we need to know about this essential standard?" or "What do we think we know about it?" If they have collected data from previous years when the same unit was taught, they might recognize common trends in student work. At this point in the process, the team is trying to determine a collective understanding of the essential skills being taught.

After answering the first PLC critical question, teams should come to a collective decision on the second question, "How will we know when students have learned it?" The PBL Learning Grid offers teams a method for organizing their answers to this question in the What do we think we know? quadrant. Having a collective understanding of what learning should look like will assist teachers in understanding what learning looks like when students are on target, approaching the target, or exceeding the target, information that will help teachers develop plans for remediating learning for students who have not reached proficiency and extending learning for students who met proficiency.

Use the "Think This, Do This" reproducible tools ("Collectively Interpret Standards" [page 111], "Examining Student Proficiency" [page 112], and "Focusing on Student Mastery" [page 113]) with collaborative teams to examine actions to take regarding focusing on results in your PLC.

Learning for All

There can be an overwhelming feeling of anxiety for teams new to these concepts of the PLC process. It is important to embrace this truth: You cannot teach every single standard. According to research, to teach all the standards, a student would need to add another 10 years to their schooling (Marzano & Kendall, 1998). Therefore, it is necessary for teacher teams to have a collective understanding of which standards are essential.

Once teams have determined that a standard is essential, they must then commit to one another and the students they serve. If it is essential for students to gain the information, then it is essential for each teacher on the team to help every student gain the essential standard. First, the team members must decide what is essential. Next, the team members must progress throughout the year, monitoring the essential standards, kid by kid and skill by skill (Eaker & Keating, 2015).

The remainder of this chapter (beginning on page 104) provides a PBL event designed to introduce participants to the concept of moving from intentions to a focus on results. While the content is used to support the main points of this chapter, the format is used to demonstrate PBL's full use of the eight elements described in chapter 3 (page 39). This PBL event is titled Learning for All. It could be utilized as a tool both for learning how to use PBL and for understanding the need for a results orientation.

Learning for All
PBL Module Facilitator Notes

This section contains background information to assist the facilitator in understanding the context of the PBL event. The purpose of this event is to introduce participants to the concept of using data to inform instruction. You will notice that the terms *PLC* and *professional learning community* are intentionally omitted from the PBL scenes. It is important to not allow previous interactions with PLC to skew participants' thinking about the fundamental concept of using data and focusing on results.

This PBL event can be conducted in a two-hour session. Read the following facilitator materials and scenes prior to beginning the session to have a complete understanding of the PBL event. Present the three scenes sequentially with discussion occurring at the close of each scene. Often, participants will pose questions after reading scene 1 that will be answered in scene 2 or 3. Recording those questions on the reproducible "PBL Learning Grid: Learning for All" (page 114) helps to reveal the learning from the scenes for the entire group.

Roles and Responsibilities

As the facilitator, your task is to manage the PBL process during the entire learning event. First, explain the group roles and how to use the PBL Learning Grid. Referring to the group roles and responsibilities in table 6.1, assign someone to serve as the manager and another person to serve as scribe. Give the individual scenes to the manager and explain that they will be leading the group discussion and should only give out one scene at a time. Stress the importance of not rushing through the scenes. They should allow enough time for the group to fully think through the problem.

TABLE 6.1: *PBL Group Roles and Responsibilities*

Group Role	Responsibility
Facilitator or mentor (Administrator, Academic Coach, or PLC Leader)	Act as a guide to ensure that all teams and individuals are fully exploring the content.
Manager	Manage the PBL process. Read each scene aloud and moderate discussions.
Scribe	Take group notes using the PBL Learning Grid and distribute information to the group.
Researcher (every participant, including manager and scribe)	Contribute to group discussions, research assigned tasks, and present findings to the group.

*Visit **go.SolutionTree.com/PLCbooks** to download a free reproducible version of this table.*

Next, groups should move to scene 1. The manager will read the scene (see reproducible page 115; scenes 2 and 3 follow on pages 116–117) with no personal interpretation, and the group will begin to analyze the problem using the PBL Learning Grid. Encourage them to summarize key information first, and then to move across the PBL Learning Grid, using it as a method of brainstorming. Make sure they are allowing enough time at the end of the session to generate learning tasks for each group member.

Take a hands-off approach as much as possible. Allow participants to struggle with concepts and direction. You may intervene with guiding questions that serve to nudge the group in the desired direction. This will most likely occur as the group answers the question, "What do we need to know?" Do not direct the problem-solving process but allow time for the group members to raise issues, discuss options, and talk about alternative solutions. Remember to keep the contents of the facilitator's portions of this guide to yourself—there are notes that are meant for your eyes only.

Introduction to the PBL Event

Unit planning can be an overwhelming task, one that involves a great deal of thought and preparation. Schools that use the PLC at Work model employ teamwork to share the load of this work. In these schools, working collaboratively is an integral part of the school culture and is accepted as the norm of operations. Furthermore, when team members appreciate the value of teaming, they celebrate the accomplishments of their collaboration and are more likely to support the learning of their students. Just as significantly, they are more likely to learn themselves, and to grow professionally in their teaching. This PBL event concludes this series of episodes with Benjamin Franklin Middle School as they continue their PLC journey.

Problem

Carla Newberry has progressed from being nervous at her new role as team lead, to feeling excitement and enthusiasm at the thought of working with her colleagues on their common goals. She has learned so much, and realizes that she is continuing to learn, just as her students are continuing to learn. She and her teammates have shared values and interests, a clear understanding of their joint mission, and have translated that into shared planning and common formative assessments of learning. Now, they have reached the point where they must work together even more closely as they prepare a remediation and enrichment plan supported by data.

Learning Objectives

The learning objectives follow the format found in the revision of Bloom's taxonomy (Armstrong, 2010). The purpose of the taxonomy is to organize learning experiences in a progression from basic knowledge, through application of the knowledge, and arriving at more complex levels of understanding, such as analysis and creative efforts. PBL events allow participants the opportunity to create new products and solutions on their own. For the Learning for All PBL event, participants will:

+ Recognize relevant student data to determine the appropriate next steps for each individual student. (Remember)
+ Compare previous remediation and enrichment plans to the newly created, individualized plans. (Understand)
+ Produce a remediation and enrichment plan, kid by kid and skill by skill, for each student. This addresses PLC critical questions three and four. (Apply)
+ Reflect on their experiences and evaluate their findings. (Analyze)

Products

The product for a PBL event is always tied to real-world applications. Such products will reflect the day-to-day practice of teaching professionals. The desired product for this PBL event reflects what happens when a team of professionals on a grade-level or content-specific team use data to plan their instruction. For the Learning for All PBL event, participants will:

+ Create a remediation and enrichment plan based on data from a recent common formative assessment.
+ Compare how they feel about sharing data to the process they just experienced, reflecting on how these actions do or do not represent the list of actions they committed to do to achieve the school's mission.

Assessments

In problem-based learning, the facilitator can use assessments to assess the progress of the group, or participants can use assessments for self-evaluation. The primary goal is for participants to evaluate their own progress and apply what they have learned on an ongoing basis. For the Learning for All PBL event:

+ The facilitator will observe and make a mental note of individual and group understanding.
+ Participants will self-assess their progress and will openly express their commitment to actions the team determines.

Table 6.2 shows the alignment between the PBL event's learning objectives, products, and assessment.

TABLE 6.2: *PBL Learning Objectives, Products, and Assessment Alignment*

Learning Objectives	Products	Assessment
(Remember) Participants will recognize relevant student data to determine the appropriate next steps for each individual student.	Teams will create a remediation and enrichment plan based on data from a recent common formative assessment.	Facilitator will observe and make a mental note of individual and group understanding.
(Understand) Participants will compare previous remediation and enrichment plans to the newly created, individualized plans.	Teams will engage in individual or whole-group discussion.	Facilitator will observe and make a mental note of individual and group understanding.
(Apply) Participants will produce a remediation and enrichment plan, kid by kid and skill by skill, for each student. This addresses PLC critical questions three and four.	Teams will create a remediation and enrichment plan based on data from a recent common formative assessment.	Facilitator will observe and make a mental note of individual and group understanding.
(Analyze) Participants will reflect on their experiences and evaluate their findings.	Individuals will compare their answers to how they feel about sharing data to the process they just experienced. They will then reflect on how these actions do or do not represent the list of actions they committed to do to achieve the mission statement.	Individuals will self-assess their progress and will openly express their commitment to these actions.

Guiding Questions

The guiding questions for each scene will help you guide participant learning. When the manager is presenting the scenes, encourage participants to work through the problem on their own, using the reproducible "PBL Learning Grid: Learning for All" (page 114). They may flounder; that is OK. Remember, the learning comes in doing the work. Allow the participants to struggle and find answers to their own questions.

If participants approach you for information, resist the urge to answer their question. Rather, present them with one of the following questions:

+ Why do you ask that question?
+ Where would you expect to find the answer to that?
+ How would you be sure that the information you find is accurate and complete?

See the reproducible "Guiding Questions for Learning for All" on page 118 for questions to use during scenes 1, 2, and 3.

Resources

Resources can take two forms, those generated by the facilitator and those the participants discover. In a professional development setting, the latter are more important than the former. The facilitator can provide a loose structure by giving participants access to well-selected resources. Understand that the more resources you provide as a facilitator, the narrower the field of exploration on the part of the participant. For this PBL event, the following resources are suggested as an appropriate starting point.

+ Eaker, R., & Keating, J. (2015). *Kid by kid, skill by skill: Teaching in a Professional Learning Community at Work.* Bloomington, IN: Solution Tree Press.
+ Eaker, R., Hagadone, M., Keating, J., & Rhoades, M. (2021). *Leading PLCs at Work districtwide: From boardroom to classroom.* Bloomington, IN: Solution Tree Press.

Time and Schedule

Every PBL event requires its own schedule; some take more time than others. Table 6.3 (page 108) is the suggested calendar for this PBL event. The time suggestions should not be construed as the only way to proceed with this event. As the facilitator, use your best judgment for how much time participants require for each activity.

TABLE 6.3: *Learning for All Schedule*

Time	Activity	Resources Needed
15 minutes	Read and discuss scene 1. Record comments on the PBL Learning Grid.	"Learning for All: Scene 1" (page 115) and "PBL Learning Grid: Learning for All" (page 114)
5 minutes	Ask participants, "Describe your feelings about sharing your students' learning data with your team members. What causes you to feel this way?"	
15 minutes	Read and discuss scene 2. Record comments on the PBL Learning Grid.	"Learning for All: Scene 2" (page 116) and "PBL Learning Grid: Learning for All" (page 114)
10 minutes	Individuals or whole groups discuss how they have formerly remediated and extended student learning after an assessment.	
15 minutes	Read and discuss scene 3. Record comments on the PBL Learning Grid.	"Learning for All: Scene 3" (page 117) and "PBL Learning Grid: Learning for All" (page 114)
20 minutes	Individuals look at student responses to the last common formative assessment given by their team. Notice the individual student responses to each skill taught. Make notes of specific trends found in the data. Next, discuss as a team their individual findings. A scribe will record findings.	CFA data, including student work
25 minutes	The team will notice what proficient student work looked like and compare it to nonproficient student work. The same process will be used for advanced level work. From this, common trends may emerge to influence the direction of the group. The team will then create a plan for addressing the needs of students who were deficient in the individual skills, the students who were on target, and those who were advanced.	CFA data, including student work
10 minutes	Team members should look at individual students and assign them to one of the three groups—below, on target, or advanced. They should develop a time for these skills to be covered and determine who will teach which items. This may look different depending on the general schedule of the school.	CFA data, including student work
5 minutes	Personal Reflection—Individuals will compare their initial feelings regarding sharing student data to the process they just experienced. They will then reflect on how these actions do (or do not) represent the list of actions they committed to do to reach the mission statement.	

THINK THIS, DO THIS
Turning Intentions Into Actions

Think This	Do This
Good intentions are important and form the foundation of why we do things. They aren't good enough, though, unless they lead to actions that then produce positive results.	☐ Reflect on the good intentions you have toward your teaching and the students you serve. ☐ Generate a prioritized set of actions that will lead to those results. ☐ Make a practice to measure results and reflect on the actions that led to those results. ☐ Make changes necessary to reach the desired results. ☐ Use evidence to drive actions rather than relying on assumptions.
Here's How	

Make a list of the intentions that guide your teaching. Reflect on each intention, writing down why each intention is important.

Next, ask yourself if and how you display those intentions in your everyday professional practice. Write down the specific actions that are required to put your intentions into use.

Create intention and action pairs.

Finally, record how you will know if you have achieved your desired results. Review this list on a weekly basis until the actions have become part of your habit of practice.

The following is an example that combines all the steps in this Think This, Do This activity.

Intentions: I intend for all of my students to learn the necessary information to move to the next level of learning. This intention is important because these students have been entrusted into my classroom for the purpose of learning specific information. It is my job to ensure that the students learn these important skills, but I cannot do this alone. I need my team members.

Displaying Intentions: To help each student learn, we must—

1. Gauge the current level of learning for each individual student.
2. Understand the learning progression of the content we are about to teach.
3. Develop formative assessments to measure the learning of the students.
4. Develop plans and then deliver the content clearly.
5. Allow each student time to take the formative assessment.
6. Analyze the results of the formative assessment.
7. Use the results to determine the next actions for helping each student learn the skills.
8. Repeat steps 2 to 7.

Intention and Action Pairs:

1. Preassess each essential skill prior to beginning a unit of study.
2. Work with my team to understand the essential standards in the unit of study.
3. Collectively develop a formative assessment to assess essential knowledge and skills.
4. Create and deliver lessons that consider individual student needs.
5. Administer the formative assessment within the team's agreed-upon window of time.
6. Analyze the assessment results individually and collectively with my team members.
7. Create and deliver remediation and enrichment to each student according to their need.

Record Desired Results: We will know this intention has been achieved when every student has learned the skill.

THINK THIS, DO THIS
Collectively Interpret Standards

Think This	Do This
Before teaching a unit, my team members and I must have a similar interpretation of the standards we are teaching.	☐ Collectively review the upcoming standards with your team members. ☐ Discuss the individual knowledge and skills the standard specifies. ☐ Come to consensus on what mastery for each knowledge and skill would look like for the standard. ☐ Ensure that all team members have a similar interpretation of each standard being taught rather than assuming.

Here's How

At the onset of each unit, review the standards associated with the upcoming unit as a team. Closely analyze each standard to determine the exact knowledge and skills associated with it.

Since standards are often interpreted differently by various readers, team members should come to a collective understanding of which knowledge and skills they will teach across all classrooms.

Once the team determines the content that they will teach, members must then specify how to measure the components of the standard. Each piece of knowledge and each individual skill must have a method of measurement so that the team can conclude to what level the students have achieved.

THINK THIS, DO THIS
Examining Student Proficiency

Think This	Do This
All students will not become proficient in a skill or concept at the same time.	☐ Analyze the assessment data for each unit by looking at every skill and every student individually. ☐ Categorize students according to their learning on the individual skill. ☐ Develop a plan to remediate or extend each student's learning according to their needs. ☐ Reteach students in different ways rather than making excuses about why students did not learn.

Here's How

After teaching a unit your team worked collaboratively to identify and plan, assess students using the method of assessment your team collectively developed. Grade the assessment using the team-developed rubric or checklist. Gather with the same group of teachers to discuss the assessment data. Rather than giving an average of grades for the entire assessment, look at each skill or concept individually on the assessment. What common patterns or mistakes are evident across multiple students' work? Did the assessment have weaknesses that contributed to student misunderstandings?

For each essential skill or concept, develop a list of students who need remediation and a list of students needing extension.

Once specific skills or concepts have emerged as needing additional practice for many students, discuss the specific methods team members used to teach the content. One or more teachers may have evidence from student assessment data to indicate the methods they used were more successful than others. Could one or more methods be helpful to use with students who need remediation or extension?

Your team may also recognize a need to research a better method for teaching the specific skill or concept. In this case, agree to gather information for teaching the topic from various sources and decide on a time to meet again and come to consensus on how to remediate and extend students on the topic.

THINK THIS, DO THIS
Focusing on Student Mastery

Think This	Do This
Teachers have a responsibility to ensure every student they serve has learned the essential skills and concepts for every subject they teach.	☐ Gather information on the learning needs of each student. ☐ Teach every student according to their specific needs. ☐ Continue teaching the essential skills and concepts until every student has learned them. ☐ If a skill or concept is essential for a student to learn, keep working with the student by reteaching and other remediation techniques until they have mastered it.

Here's How

Refer to the list your team previously developed of students in need of remediation for a specific skill or concept. Determine which teacher will remediate the individual students and the time for this remediation to occur.

Collect formative data on the students' learning during the instruction. Track their progress and report your findings at the next team meeting.

Continue the previous cycle of discussing data and developing a plan of action. Do this until each student has gained mastery of the essential skills and concepts.

PBL Learning Grid: Learning for All

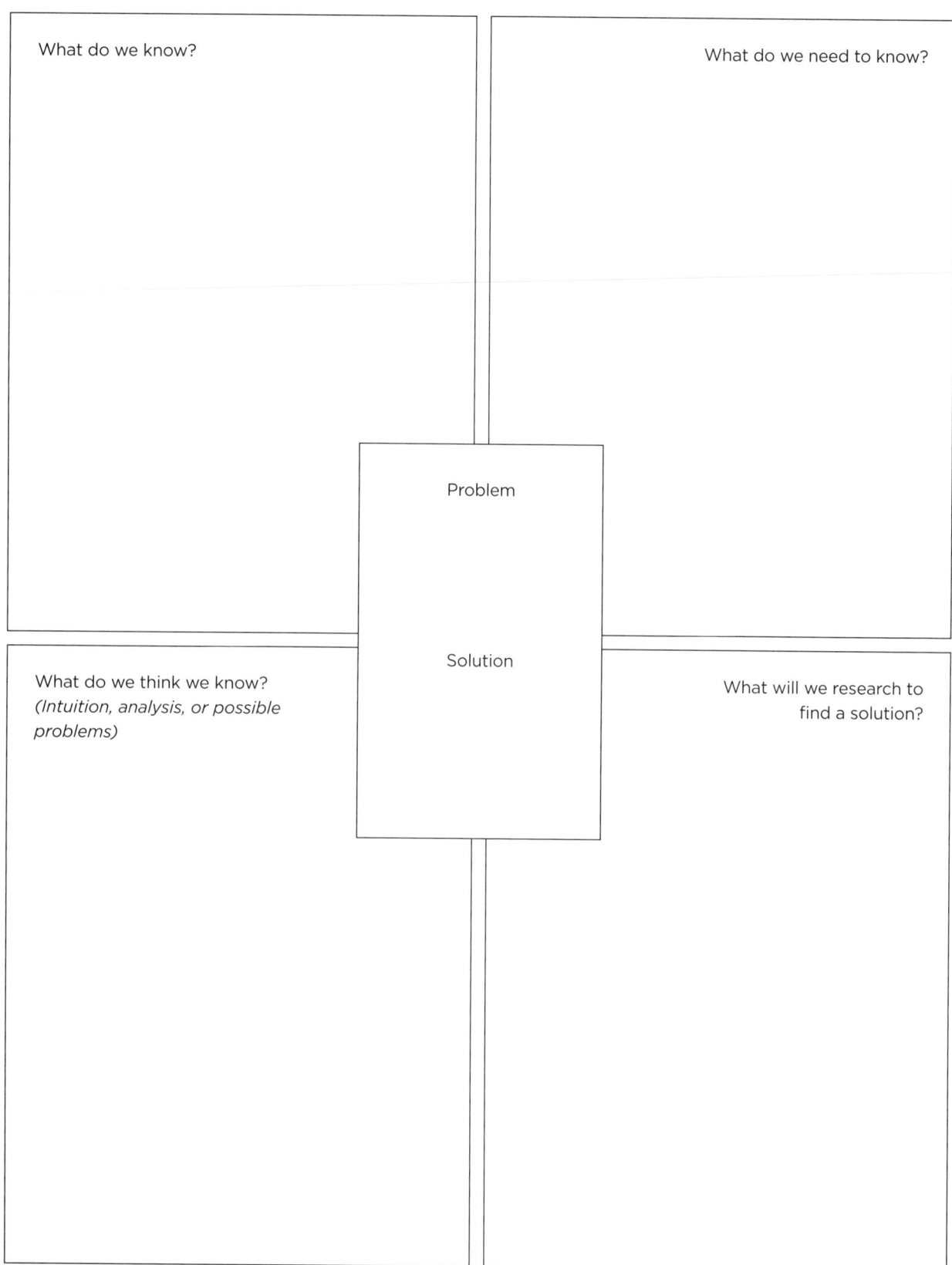

| What do we know? | What do we need to know? |

| What do we think we know? *(Intuition, analysis, or possible problems)* | What will we research to find a solution? |

Problem

Solution

Learning for All: Scene 1

With each passing day, Carla Newberry was growing fonder of the opportunities to meet with her colleagues. Walking into Principal Kindred's conference room for the bimonthly leadership meeting, she had the sense that others felt the same way. Everyone gathered into the room sharing pleasantries, but Principal Kindred was quick to begin the meeting on time. After reviewing the norms, Mrs. Goodwin spoke up, "You know, when we first started this work, I thought stating the norms at the beginning of the meeting was juvenile and unnecessary. But now, I appreciate them because I think it reminds everyone that we are professionals and the work we are about to begin is important."

"I haven't really thought about it that way, but I can see your point," replied Mr. Lawson. "Before, we were all friendly with one another. When we would meet in years past, the time was not always spent in professional ways. Stating the norms sets the tone."

"Setting the tone is going to be important as we really dig into this work. As we all learn how to use our assessment data to inform our practice, we have to approach the work in a positive way," Principal Kindred shared, as he steered the conversation to the first agenda item. "Talk to me about writing your first common formative assessment," he said.

"Well, um, it was a little difficult," began Mrs. Goodwin. "The science department struggled a bit to have *everyone* understand why we needed to make a common assessment."

"That is OK. And it is understandable. People need to understand why they are being asked to do something that can be very time consuming," replied Principal Kindred. "I will make a plan to be clearer in describing that to the faculty," he continued.

"I had some teachers questioning if it would be acceptable to simply take a ready-made test by the textbook manufacturer," Mr. Lawson stated. "Our math book has great questions with fabulous graphics," he explained. A conversation continued about how to resolve that question. Before moving on to the next agenda item, Principal Kindred reminded the group, "Let's never forget that the power is in the doing. We learn by doing. When we learn collectively, then we learn more." There were many nods of agreement as team members began writing in their notepads.

"Data is just data, until you do something with it," Principal Kindred continued. "We are only going to see student learning improve if we take the data we collect from this first common formative assessment and use it to develop our upcoming remediation and extension plans," he said. "I would like to spend the rest of this meeting equipping ourselves to face the common pitfalls observed by those who have done this process successfully." At this, Principal Kindred motioned around the room to several large pieces of paper posted on the walls. Each page contained only a word or phrase at the top. "I want to take these issues one by one and develop a common response as to why these will not prevent us from doing what research has proven is the correct course of action. Mr. Norris, can I call on you to be the first scribe?" Principal Kindred asked. Rising to his feet, Rick Norris replied, "Absolutely!"

"Since you are first, I will let you choose the first topic. Which one would you like to discuss?" Principal Kindred asked.

Learning for All: Scene 2

The team members were sitting in a circle, each holding three sheets of paper. Carla asked, "Are you ready to do this?" "Just rip off the Band-Aid," Trent replied. "Let's do it," said Michelle. With that, the three distributed their assessment data from their first common formative assessment. In the past four weeks, these veteran teachers had spent more time working with one another than they had in the previous five years combined.

"Oh, thank goodness!" said Michelle, breaking the silence. "I have spent all night scared to see your data in fear that my scores were much lower than both of yours." Nodding, Trent said, "I considered taking a sick day today."

Carla spoke up. "When I was in the team leader training, they stressed how important it is for us to understand that teaching is really 'not about us, it just involves us.'"

"I have heard Principal Kindred say that too, and I think it's a good way of putting it," replied Trent. He continued, "It helps me to focus on student learning, but it can still be intimidating. I want the best for my students. What can I do that's different and better?"

Carla replied, "Well, let's look at the test results. They give us information we need about the current learning of each student. With this, we can make decisions that can significantly impact their learning."

"But what decisions can we make?" asked Michelle. "I taught these lessons the best way I know how. I am not sure what to do differently for remediation," she continued. "Exactly!" said Trent. "It is just so frustrating when you teach your heart out and then they don't get it."

Carla paused, and then said, "Let's try to just look at it skill by skill. We should look at individual data for the first skill on the assessment. We had four questions for that skill. Let's look at these four questions and see if anything sticks out." They all read silently for a few minutes. "Are you noticing that many students who missed question two also missed question three?" asked Trent. "Yes," replied Michelle, "and many of mine who missed it selected choice C. I can see why they would make that mistake."

After a brief discussion, Carla stated, "We need to make a list of the students who scored proficient on this skill, those who were below proficient, and those above proficient." The team continued through this process until they had lists for each skill on the assessment.

"So now is where the rubber meets the road. Do you trust me enough to allow me some time each day with your students?" Carla asked. "Do *I* trust *you* enough to do the same thing with my students? If we really want to be efficient, then each one of us will take one of these lists and teach the students the necessary information during remediation and extension time this week."

After a brief silence, Trent spoke first, "I don't think we have any other choice." Pointing to the sign in his room, he said, "If we want learning for all, then we have to do what is best for students, not what's easiest for us."

Michelle smiled and said, "Where do we begin?"

Learning for All: Scene 3

"Can we have a quick meeting in my room after school at 3:15 p.m. today?" read the email from Trent. Carla noticed he had sent it to her and Michelle at 1:25 p.m. that day—right after remediation and extension. She wondered if something bad happened. She tried not to allow her mind to wander as she taught her last block of the day, but she could not help but worry about the impromptu meeting. She tried to recall which students from her roster were on his list. If Marcus and Logan were both on his list, then they may have given him trouble, she thought. No, Marcus was in the extension group, and Trent was working with the remedial group. Maybe it was the lesson, she thought. He might not have liked how the lesson went and wants advice on how to change it before tomorrow.

When the 3:15 bell rang, she met Michelle in the hall as they were both walking into Trent's room. "Well, what did you guys think?" he asked excitedly. "About what?" Carla asked. "Remediation and extension," he replied. "The group I had was great! I think we made some important connections."

"That is awesome," said Michelle. "I could see a lot of positive things from the students as well. It was helpful having them together. We have terrific students! I think they appreciated the fact that we were using the time to extend their learning."

"Yes. I think so too!" Trent replied. "And I am over here having some aha moments. All this time, I have been thinking of this process wrong. I would teach the material, test the material, and then move on. I was always so frustrated with the process. I think we truly can know if the students are getting the information."

Excitedly, Carla said, "That is wonderful, Trent! I am so glad you are seeing this as an achievable task. I don't think it is going to be easy, but together we *can* ensure learning for all."

Guiding Questions for Learning for All

Scene 1

1. What are some of the reasons that teachers give for not using data more often to inform their practice?

2. Where could you go to find reliable information to address these concerns?

3. How can we work together to address these issues?

Scene 2

1. What do the teachers mean by saying they are going to trust each other with their students?

2. How does this relate to the principles and practices of a PLC?

3. What do you notice about the relationship between the team members?

4. What do you think about the teachers' attitudes toward their practice?

Mindset for Success © 2025 Solution Tree Press • SolutionTree.com
Visit **go.SolutionTree.com/PLCBooks** to download this free reproducible.

Scene 3

1. How has Carla's team changed over the course of the episodes?

2. What do you think could have gone wrong when the team shared students during their remediation and extension time?

3. What could have gone right with sharing students?

4. What type of connections might have been made in the remediation and extension groups?

5. Where do you think Trent is now when he explains that he used to "do it all wrong"? How did he get there?

Final Reflection

1. Reflect on what you learned, not just about how to focus on results and examine and use data, but on the process you used to identify the problem and how to solve it.

Epilogue

This book will close just as it opened, considering Watty Piper's (2020) book *The Little Engine That Could*; however, now we can look at the story with a PBL mindset. The Little Engine identified the problem quickly. There was no engine to take the train over the mountain. She could have been distracted by the other problems that were out of her control. The children would be disappointed if the toys did not arrive. The food on the train was probably going to spoil. These issues carried a whole host of other potential problems. Regardless, the problem within her control was moving the train. There were things that she did not know. She did not know how to get over the mountain or what she would encounter once she arrived. Those unknowns did not stop her from trying. She used action research to learn how to pull and how to tug with the correct amount of force to move the train. Because she thought she could, she put forth the actions necessary to deliver the toys and food to the children on the other side of the mountain. The Little Engine's PBL Learning Grid might have looked something like the one in figure E.1 (page 122).

Our goal with this book has been to guide school leaders, team leaders, teacher leaders, and others in helping teams understand how to "think this, do this." We can have the greatest of intentions, but if we don't put them into action, they are useless to us. People go to conferences and get excited, but then come home to the same challenges and soon lose the fire that started when they were "thinking this." We must shift our thinking from the abstract to the concrete, from good ideas to great actions, and often this begins with attempts.

As teachers, we have a decision to make. Will we be willing or unwilling participants in the education path we have chosen as our profession? Will we, like the Little Engine, *think we can* and then do the work necessary to persevere? Or will we make excuses like the other three engines and refuse to try? The Little Engine truly had a mindset for success. The question we must ask ourselves is, Can we have this mindset? The answer is, Yes! We think we can!

What did the Little Engine know? A train carrying a load of toys and food needed to get over the mountain. She was not very big. She had never been over the mountain or carried such a heavy load.	**What did the Little Engine need to know?** How do you get over the mountain? What is on the other side of the mountain?
What did the Little Engine think she knew? She thought she could pull the train over the mountain.	**What did the Little Engine research to find a solution to the problem?** She considered how she could pull and tug the train.

Problem
There was no engine to take the train over the mountain.

Solution
Think you can and try hard until you do.

FIGURE E.1: *PBL Learning Grid for the Little Engine.*

References and Resources

Ainsworth, L. (2015). *Common formative assessments 2.0: How teacher teams intentionally align standards, instruction, and assessment.* Thousand Oaks, CA: Corwin Press.

Albanese, M. A., & Mitchell, S. (1993). "Problem-based learning: A review of literature on its outcomes and implementation issues": Correction. *Academic Medicine, 68*(8), 615.

AllThingsPLC. (n.d.). *See the evidence.* Accessed at https://allthingsplc.info/evidence on March 10, 2024.

Armstrong, P. (2010). *Bloom's taxonomy.* Vanderbilt University Center for Teaching. Accessed at https://cft.vanderbilt.edu/guides-sub-pages/blooms-taxonomy on August 18, 2023.

Bandura, A. (1977). Self-efficacy: Toward a unifying theory of behavioral change. *Psychological Review, 84*(2), 191–215.

Bandura, A. (1997). *Self-efficacy: The exercise of control.* New York: W. H. Freeman.

Barrows, H. (1994). *Practice-based learning: Problem-based learning applied to medical education.* Springfield, IL: Southern Illinois University School of Medicine.

Barrows, H. (1996). Problem-based learning in medicine and beyond: A brief overview. *New Directions for Teaching and Learning, 68,* 3–12.

Barrows, H. (2000). *Problem-based learning applied to medical education.* Springfield, IL: Southern Illinois University School of Medicine.

Barrows, H., & Pickell, G. (1991). *Developing clinical problem-solving skills: A guide to more effective diagnosis and treatment.* New York: W. W. Norton.

Bayewitz, M. D., Cunningham, S. A., Ianora, J. A., Jones, B., Nielsen, M., Remmert, W., et al. (2020). *Help your team: Overcoming common collaborative challenges in a PLC at Work.* Bloomington, IN: Solution Tree Press.

Bernhardt, V. L. (2018). *Data analysis for continuous school improvement.* New York: Routledge.

Bhatt, J., & Swick, M. (2017, March 15). *Focusing on teamwork and communication to improve patient safety* [Blog post]. Accessed at www.aha.org/news/blog/2017-03-15-focusing-teamwork-and-communication-improve-patient-safety on July 15, 2022.

Black, P., & Wiliam, D. (1998). Assessment and classroom learning. *Assessment in Education: Principles, Policy & Practice, 5*(1), 7–74.

Blanchard, K. (2009). *Leading at a higher level: Blanchard on leadership and creating high performing organizations.* Upper Saddle River, NJ: FT Press.

Bloom, B. S. (Ed.). (1956). *Taxonomy of educational objectives: The classification of educational goals; Handbook I: Cognitive domain.* New York: McKay.

Boogren, T. H. (2018). *The beginning teacher's field guide: Embarking on your first years*. Bloomington, IN: Solution Tree Press.

Bowman, J. (2007). *Honor: A history*. New York: Encounter Books.

BrainyQuote. (n.d.). *Ralph Waldo Emerson quotes*. Accessed at www.brainyquote.com/quotes/ralph_waldo_emerson_108797 on July 5, 2024.

Bransford, J. D. (1997). *The Jasper project: Lessons in curriculum, instruction, assessment, and professional development*. New York: Routledge.

Bridges, E. M. (1992). *Problem-based learning for administrators*. Eugene, OR: ERIC Clearinghouse on Educational Management.

Bridges, E. M., & Hallinger, P. (1995). *Implementing problem-based learning in leadership development*. Eugene, OR: ERIC Clearinghouse on Educational Management.

Brown, P. C., Roediger, H. L., III, & McDaniel, M. A. (2014). *Make it stick: The science of successful learning*. Cambridge, MA: Belknap Press.

Bryant, A. (2014, January 4). Management be nimble. *The New York Times*. Accessed at www.nytimes.com/2014/01/05/business/management-be-nimble.html on March 8, 2024.

Buffum, A., Mattos, M., & Weber, C. (2009). *Pyramid response to intervention: RTI, professional learning communities, and how to respond when kids don't learn*. Bloomington, IN: Solution Tree Press.

Buffum, A., Mattos, M., & Weber, C. (2012). *Simplifying response to intervention: Four essential guiding principles*. Bloomington, IN: Solution Tree Press.

Carter, J. L., & Krahenbuhl, K. S. (2022). *Teaching signature thinking: Strategies for unleashing creativity in the classroom*. New York: Routledge.

Chenoweth, K. (2009). It can be done, it's being done, and here's how. *Phi Delta Kappan, 91*(1), 38–43.

Clouse, R. W., Goodin, T., & Aniello, J. (2016). Entrepreneurs in action! An authentic learning experience. In M. H. Morris & E. Liguori (Eds.), *Annals of entrepreneurship education and pedagogy–2016* (pp. 246–273). Northampton, MA: Elgar.

Collins, J. (2001). *Good to great: Why some companies make the leap. . . and others don't*. New York: HarperCollins.

Conzemius, A. E., & O'Neill, J. (2014). *The handbook for SMART school teams: Revitalizing best practices for collaboration* (2nd ed.). Bloomington, IN: Solution Tree Press.

Copland, M. (2000). Problem-based learning and prospective principals' problem-framing ability. *Educational Administration Quarterly, 36*(4), 585–607.

Cottingham, B. W., Hough, H. J., & Myung, J. (2023). *What does it take to accelerate the learning of every child? Early insights from a CCEE school-improvement pilot*. Stanford, CA: Policy Analysis for California Education. Accessed at https://edpolicyinca.org/sites/default/files/2023-12/r_cottingham-dec2023.pdf on April 1, 2024.

Couros, G. (2015). *The innovator's mindset: Empower learning, unleash talent, and lead a culture of creativity*. San Diego, CA: Dave Burgess Consulting.

Dewey, J. (1938). *Experience and education*. New York: Free Press.

Dillard, H. (2012). *The effects of professional learning communities on the efficacy level of novice teachers: A mixed methods study* [Doctoral dissertation, Tennessee State University]. ProQuest. http://search.proquest.com/docview/1017706439 on April 16, 2024.

Dillard, H. (2016). Pre-service training in professional learning communities benefits novice teacher. *Transformative Dialogues: Teaching & Learning, 9*(2), 1–13.

Dillard, H. (2019). The power of norms. *AllThingsPLC Magazine, 3*(3), 36–41.

Dillard, H. (2024). Professionals learning in community: The most effective PD model. *AllThingsPLC Magazine, 8*(1), 46–47.

Doerr, J. (2017). *Measure what matters: How Google, Bono, and the Gates Foundation rock the world with OKRs*. New York: Portfolio/Penguin.

Donohoo, J., Hattie, J., & Eells, R. (2018). The power of collective efficacy. *Educational Leadership, 75*(6), 40–44.

DuFour, R., DuFour, R., & Eaker, R. (2008). *Revisiting Professional Learning Communities at Work: New insights for improving schools*. Bloomington, IN: Solution Tree Press.

DuFour, R., DuFour, R., Eaker, R., Many, T. W., & Mattos, M. (2016). *Learning by doing: A handbook for Professional Learning Communities at Work* (3rd ed.). Bloomington, IN: Solution Tree Press.

DuFour, R., DuFour, R., Eaker, R., Many, T., Mattos, M., & Muhammad, A. (2024). *Learning by doing: A handbook for Professional Learning Communities at Work* (4th ed.). Bloomington, IN: Solution Tree Press.

DuFour, R., DuFour, R., Eaker, R., Mattos, M., & Muhammed, A. (2021). *Revisiting Professional Learning Communities at Work: Proven insights for sustained, substantive school improvement* (2nd ed.). Bloomington, IN: Solution Tree Press.

DuFour, R., & Eaker, R. (1998). *Professional Learning Communities at Work: Best practices for enhancing student achievement*. Bloomington, IN: Solution Tree Press.

DuFour, R., & Marzano, R. (2011). *Leaders of learning: How district, school, and classroom leaders improve student achievement*. Bloomington, IN: Solution Tree Press.

DuFour, R., & Reeves, D. (2016). The futility of PLC lite. *Phi Delta Kappan, 97*(6), 69–71.

Dweck, C. (2006). *Mindset: The new psychology of success*. New York: Ballantine.

Eaker, R., Hagadone, M., Keating, J., & Rhoades, M. (2021). *Leading PLCs at Work districtwide: From boardroom to classroom*. Bloomington, IN: Solution Tree Press.

Eaker, R., & Keating, J. (2015). *Kid by kid, skill by skill: Teaching in a Professional Learning Community at Work*. Bloomington, IN: Solution Tree Press.

Edmondson, A. C. (2013, December 17). *The three pillars of a teaming culture*. Accessed at https://hbr.org/2013/12/the-three-pillars-of-a-teaming-culture on June 10, 2023.

Freiberg, K., & Freiberg, J. (1997). *Nuts! Southwest Airlines' crazy recipe for business and personal success*. New York: Broadway Books.

Fullan, M. (2001). *Leading in a culture of change*. San Francisco: Jossey-Bass.

Fullan, M. (2005). *Leadership and sustainability: System thinkers in action*. Thousand Oaks, CA: Corwin Press.

Fulton, K., & Britton, T. (2011, June). *STEM teachers in professional learning communities: From good teachers to great teaching*. Washington, DC: National Commission on Teaching and America's Future. Accessed at https://www2.wested.org/www-static/online_pubs/1098-executive-summary.pdf on March 8, 2024.

Glasgow, N. A. (1997). *New curriculum for new times: A guide to student-centered, problem-based learning*. Thousand Oaks, CA: Corwin Press.

Goodin, T. (2003). *Evaluating the entrepreneurship education initiative: Entrepreneurs in action*. Nashville, TN: Peabody College for Teachers of Vanderbilt University.

Goodin, T., Caukin, N., & Dillard, H. (2019). Developing clinical reasoning skills in teacher candidates using a problem-based learning approach. *Interdisciplinary Journal of Problem-Based Learning, 13*(1).

Gordon, P. R., Rogers, A. M., Comfort, M., Gavula, N., & McGee, B. P. (2001). A taste of problem-based learning increases achievement of urban minority middle-school students. *Educational Horizons, 79*(4), 171–175.

Greenwood, B. (Guest). (2020, October 21). Episode 68 – Thinking differently to grow your business [Audio podcast episode]. In *ASA Podcast*. Accessed at https://members.asashop.org/asa-podcasts/Details/episode-68-thinking-differently-to-grow-your-business-42038 on July 15, 2022.

Hallinger, P., Jiafang, L. & Showanasai, P. (2019). Seeing and hearing is believing, but eating is knowing: A case study of implementing PBL in a master of educational management program. In M. Moallem, W. Hung & N. Dabbagh (Eds.), *Wiley Handbook of Problem Based Learning* (pp. 483–506). New York: John Wiley & Sons.

Hanson, H., Torres, K., Yoon, S. Y., Merrill, R., Fantz, T., & Velie, Z. (2021). *Growing together: Professional Learning Communities at Work generates achievement gains in Arkansas*. Portland, OR: Education Northwest. Accessed at https://educationnorthwest.org/sites/default/files/plc-at-work-impact-evaluation.pdf on April 1, 2024.

Hattie, J. (2012). *Visible learning for teachers: Maximizing impact on learning.* New York: Routledge.

Hattie, J. (2015, October 27). We aren't using assessments correctly. *Education Week.* Accessed at www.edweek.org/policy-politics/opinion-we-arent-using-assessments-correctly/2015/10 on August 1, 2023.

Hayes, M., Chumney, F., Wright, C., & Buckingham, M. (2019). *The global study of engagement: A technical report.* Roseland, NJ: ADP Research Institute. Accessed at www.adpri.org/wp-content/uploads/2020/07/R0101_0718_v2_GE_ResearchReport.pdf on March 8, 2024.

Hmelo, C. E., Gotterer, G. S., & Bransford, J. D. (1997). A theory-driven approach to assessing the cognitive effects of PBL. *Instructional Science, 25,* 387–408. https://doi.org/10.1023/A:1003013126262

Hyatt, M. (2018). *Your best year ever: A 5-step plan for achieving your most important goals.* Grand Rapids, MI: Baker Books.

Hyatt, M. (2020). *The vision-driven leader: 10 questions to focus your efforts, energize your team, and scale your business.* Grand Rapids, MI: Baker Books.

Imagination Library. (2020, March 30). *The Imagination Library presents "goodnight with Dolly".* Accessed at https://imaginationlibrary.com/goodnight-with-dolly-read-aloud on May 26, 2023.

Kahneman, D. (2011). *Thinking, fast and slow.* New York: Farrar, Straus and Giroux.

Kanold, T. D. (2011). *The five disciplines of PLC leaders.* Bloomington, IN: Solution Tree Press.

Kanold, T. D. (2017). *HEART! Fully forming your professional life as a teacher and leader.* Bloomington, IN: Solution Tree Press.

Katzenbach, J. R., & Smith, D. K. (1993). *The wisdom of teams: Creating the high-performance organization.* Boston: Harvard Business School Press.

Kegan, R., & Lahey, L. L. (2001). *How the way we talk can change the way we work: Seven languages for transformation.* San Francisco: Jossey-Bass.

King, J. (2019, November 29). How great leaders communicate big vision so that others want to join in. *Medium.* Accessed at https://medium.com/@Jude.M/how-great-leaders-communicate-big-vision-so-that-others-want-to-join-in-d3296e7ca37e on August 11, 2023.

Klein, A. (2021). *1,500 Decisions a day (at least!): How teachers cope with a dizzying array of questions.* Accessed at www.edweek.org/teaching-learning/1-500-decisions-a-day-at-least-how-teachers-cope-with-a-dizzying-array-of-questions/2021/12 on August 1, 2024.

Kohn, A. (1988). *Beyond selfishness.* Accessed at www.alfiekohn.org/article/beyond-selfishness on July 10, 2023.

Kouzes, J., & Posner, B. (1999). *Encouraging the heart: A leader's guide to rewarding and recognizing others.* San Francisco: Jossey-Bass.

Lambros, A. (2002). *Problem-based learning in K–8 classrooms: A teacher's guide to implementation.* Thousand Oaks, CA: Corwin Press.

Landsberg, M. (2002). *The Tao of coaching: Boost your effectiveness at work by inspiring and developing those around you.* London: Profile Books.

leap4principals. (2018, August 11). *John Hattie - Collective teacher efficacy 2018* [Video file]. Accessed at www.youtube.com/watch?v=UCMV692itfg on August 1, 2023.

Lencioni, P. (2002). *The five dysfunctions of a team: A leadership fable.* San Francisco: Jossey-Bass.

Lezotte, L. W. (n.d.). *Revolutionary and evolutionary: The effective schools movement.* Accessed at www.brjonesphd.com/uploads/1/6/9/4/16946150/revolutionary_and_evolutionary-_the_effective_schools_movement_-_dr._lawrence_w._lezotte.pdf on July 10, 2023.

Many, T., Maffoni, M., Sparks, S., & Thomas, T. (2018). *Amplify your impact: Coaching collaborative teams in PLCs at Work.* Bloomington, IN: Solution Tree Press.

Martin, M. (2019, September 24). *90th anniversary edition of "The Little Engine That Could" with introduction by Dolly Parton.* Accessed at https://dollyparton.com/tag/the-little-engine-that-could on May 26, 2023.

Marzano, R. J., & Kendall, J. S. (1998). *Awash in a sea of standards.* Accessed at https://cdnsm5-ss11.sharpschool.com/UserFiles/Servers/Server_610718/File/Academics/Curriculum/5982IR_AwashInASea.pdf on August 25, 2023.

Marzano, R. J., Warrick, P., & Simms, J. A. (2014). *A handbook for high reliability schools: The next step in school reform*. Bloomington, IN: Marzano Resources.

Mattos, M., & Buffum, A. (Eds.). (2015). *It's about time: Planning interventions and extensions in secondary school*. Bloomington, IN: Solution Tree Press.

Mattos, M., DuFour, R., DuFour, R., Eaker, R., & Many, T. (2016). *Concise answers to frequently asked questions about Professional Learning Communities at Work*. Bloomington, IN: Solution Tree Press.

Maxwell, N. L., Bellisimo, Y., & Mergendoller, J. (2001). Problem-based learning: Modifying the medical school model for teaching high school economics. *The Social Studies, 92*(2), 73–78.

McGonigal, K. (2012). *The willpower instinct: How self-control works, why it matters, and what you can do to get more of it*. New York: Avery.

Michael Jr. (2017, January 8). *Know your why* [Video file]. Accessed at www.youtube.com/watch?v=1ytFB8TrkTo on August 1, 2023.

National Academies of Sciences, Engineering, and Medicine. (2018). *How people learn II: Learners, contexts, and cultures*. Washington, DC: The National Academies Press.

Patterson, K., Grenny, J., McMillan, R., & Switzler, A. (2002). *Crucial conversations: Tools for talking when stakes are high*. New York: McGraw-Hill.

Peters, T., & Waterman, R. (1982). *In search of excellence: Lessons from America's best-run companies*. New York: Harper & Row.

Pfeffer, J., & Sutton, R. I. (2000). *The knowing-doing gap: How smart companies turn knowledge into action*. Boston: Harvard Business School Press.

Pinchot, G., & Pinchot, E. (1993). *The end of bureaucracy and the rise of the intelligent organization*. San Francisco: Berrett-Koehler.

Piper, W. (2020). *The little engine that could* (90th anniversary ed.). New York: Grosset & Dunlap.

Popham, W. J. (2013, January 8). *Waving the flag for formative assessment*. Accessed at www.edweek.org/teaching-learning/opinion-waving-the-flag-for-formative-assessment/2013/01 on March 8, 2024.

Practice. (n.d.). In *Merriam-Webster's online dictionary*. Accessed at www.merriam-webster.com/dictionary/practice on July 18, 2024.

Ragland, M. A., Clubine, B., Constable, D., & Smith, P. A. (2002, April). *Expecting success: A study of five high performing, high poverty schools*. Washington, DC: Council of Chief State School Officers. Accessed at https://files.eric.ed.gov/fulltext/ED468010.pdf on March 8, 2024.

Read On Arizona. (n.d.). *Case studies: Agua Caliente Elementary and Tanque Verde Elementary*. Accessed at https://readonarizona.org/case-studies/TVUSD on April 1, 2024.

Reeves, D. B. (2006). *The learning leader: How to focus school improvement for better results*. Alexandria, VA: ASCD.

Reeves, D., & Eaker, R. (2019). *100-day leaders: Turning short-term wins into long-term success in schools*. Bloomington, IN: Solution Tree Press.

Schmoker, M. (2004). Learning communities at the crossroads: Toward the best schools we've ever had. *Phi Delta Kappan, 86*(1), 84–89.

Schwartz, K. (2017, June 14). *How do you know when a teaching strategy is most effective? John Hattie has an idea*. Accessed at www.kqed.org/mindshift/48112/how-do-you-know-when-a-teaching-strategy-is-most-effective-john-hattie-has-an-idea on August 11, 2023.

Seifert, E. H., & Simmons, D. (1997). Learning centered schools using a problem-based approach. *NASSP Bulletin, 81*(587), 90–97.

Senge, P. M. (1990). *The fifth discipline: The art and practice of the learning organization*. New York: Doubleday.

Senge, P. M., Kleiner, A., Roberts, C., Ross, R. B., & Smith, B. J. (1994). *The fifth discipline fieldbook: Strategies and tools for building a learning organization*. New York: Doubleday.

Solution Tree. (n.d.a). *Evidence of excellence: Greater Hartford Academy of the Arts Middle School*. Accessed at www.solutiontree.com/plc-at-work/evidence-of-excellence/greater-hartford-academy on April 1, 2024.

Solution Tree. (n.d.b). *Evidence of excellence: Minnieville Elementary School*. Accessed at www.solutiontree.com /plc-at-work/evidence-of-excellence/minnieville on April 1, 2024.

Solution Tree. (n.d.c). *Evidence of excellence: Model PLC at Work and Blue Ribbon Schools*. Accessed at www .solutiontree.com/plc-at-work/evidence-of-excellence/model-plc-and-blue-ribbon-schools on April 1, 2024.

Solution Tree. (n.d.d). *Evidence of excellence: Pasadena Independent School District*. Accessed at www.solutiontree .com/plc-at-work/evidence-of-excellence/pasadena on April 1, 2024.

Stanley, A. (2020, August 3). *Leading through, part 3: Leading with clarity* [Video file]. Accessed at www.youtube .com/watch?v=5ahJVfHMfhc on August 10, 2023.

Stepien, W. J., Gallagher, S. A., & Workman, D. (1993). Problem-based learning for traditional and interdisciplinary classrooms. *Journal for the Education of the Gifted, 16*(4), 338–357.

Tschannen-Moran, M. (2014). *Trust matters: Leadership for successful schools* (2nd ed.). San Francisco: Jossey-Bass.

Torres, K., Rooney, K., Holmgren, M., Yoon, S. Y., Taylor, S., & Hanson, H. (2021). *PLC at Work in Arkansas: Driving achievement results through school transformation and innovation*. Portland, OR: Education Northwest.

Vernon, D. T., & Blake, R. L. (1993). Does problem-based learning work? A meta-analysis of evaluative research. *Academic Medicine, 68*(7), 550–563.

Vye, N. J., Goldman, S. R., Voss, J. F., Hmelo, C., & Williams, S. (1997). Complex mathematical problem solving by individuals and dyads. *Cognition and Instruction, 15*(4), 435–484.

Waack, S. (2018, May 7). Collective Teacher Efficacy (CTE) according to John Hattie. *Visible Learning*. Accessed at https://visible-learning.org/2018/03/collective-teacher-efficacy-hattie on May 26, 2023.

Walton, H. J., & Matthews, M. B. (1989). Essentials of problem-based learning. *Medical Education, 23*(6), 542–558.

Wiliam, D., & Thompson, M. (2007). Integrating assessment with instruction: What will it take to make it work? In C. A. Dwyer (Ed.), *The future of assessment: Shaping teaching and learning* (pp. 53–82). New York: Routledge.

Williams, T., Perry, M., Studier, C., Brazil, N., Kirst, M., Haertel, E., et al. (2005, October). *Similar students, different results: Why do some schools do better?* Moutain View, CA: EdSource. Accessed at https://edsource.org /wp-content/uploads/2019/06/SimStu_10-2005.pdf on April 15, 2024.

Willpower. (n.d.a). In *Cambridge online dictionary*. Accessed at https://dictionary.cambridge.org/dictionary/english /willpower on April 14, 2024.

Willpower. (n.d.b). In *Merriam-Webster's online dictionary*. Accessed at www.merriam-webster.com/dictionary /willpower on July 18, 2024.

Wise, B. (2016, June 4). *Remembering Muhammad Ali, 'the greatest of all time,' by his 10 greatest quotes*. Accessed at www .cbssports.com/boxing/news/remembering-muhammad-ali-the-greatest-of-all-time-by-his-10-greatest-quotes on March 8, 2024.

Yeager, D. S., & Dweck, C. S. (2020). What can be learned from growth mindset controversies? *American Psychologist, 75*(9), 1269–1284. https://doi.org/10.1037/amp0000794

Yousafzai, M. (2014). *I am Malala: How one girl stood up for education and changed the world*. New York: Little, Brown & Company.

Yew, E. H. J., & Goh, K. (2016). Problem-based learning: An overview of its process and impact on learning. *Health Professions Education, 2*(2), 75–79.

Zak, P. (2017, January-February). The neuroscience of trust. *Harvard Business Review*, 84–90.

Zull, J. (2002). *The art of changing the brain: Enriching the practice of teaching by exploring the biology of learning*. New York: Routledge.

Index

A
adult learners, xvi, 10
Ali, M., 10
assessments
    and decision making within the school system, 101–102
    elements of the PBL method, 46–47
    Fundamentals: PBL module facilitator notes, 63
    Learning for All: PBL module facilitator notes, 106
    Writing on the Wall: PBL module facilitator notes, 83

B
behaviors to build better job performance, 24
Bernhardt, V., 58
Black, P., 28
Bridges, E., 42
building a powerful partnership: PLC at Work and PBL. *See also* problem-based learning (PBL); Professional Learning Communities at Work (PLCs at Work)
    about, 9–10
    balance and trust, 15–16
    changes in thinking, 14–15
    heart, head, and hands, 16–17
    problem-based learning methods, 12–14
    professional learning communities, 11–12
    theory and practice, 15
building collaborative skill power: problem-based learning. *See also* problem-based learning (PBL)
    about, 39
    bridge between learning and practice, 42–43
    elements of the PBL method, 43–48
    example learning grid for PLCs, 50–51
    from method to mindset, 51–52
    PBL Learning Grid, 48–50
    reproducibles for, 53
    roots of PBL, 39–42
building collaborative willpower: learning to trust the PLC process using PBL. *See also* problem-based learning (PBL); Professional Learning Communities at Work (PLCs at Work)
    about, 19
    PLC LIGHT, 19–25
    reproducibles for, 30–37
    strength in numbers, 29
    trustworthy process and PLC process, 25–29

C
collaboration. *See also* shifting from isolation to collaboration
    decision making within the school system, 101–103
    definition of, 77
    focus on, 80
    interdependence and, 78–79
    systematic process of, 78
collaborative teams
    elements of the PBL method and, 43, 47
    focus on collaboration, 80
    PBL Learning Grid and, 50, 51–52
    in a PLC, xvi–xvii, 2, 58–60
    PLC LIGHT and, 20, 21, 22–25
    strength in numbers, 29
    system of interventions and extensions, 28
    working collectively on specific items, 79–80
collective teacher efficacy, 2, 25–26
commitments
    clarifying commitments, 26–27
    values (collective commitments), 57, 59
common formative assessments, 21, 22, 28, 102. *See also* assessments

D
decision fatigue, 3
decision making
    evidence-based decision making, 28–29
    within the school system, 101–103
    using data, 100–101
DRIP, 100
DuFour, R., 2, 58
DuFour, R., 2, 58
dynamic PBL, 42. *See also* problem-based learning (PBL)

E

Eaker, R., 2, 58
Emerson, R., 16
essential standards and acting with intention, 103. *See also* standards
evidence-based decision making, 28–29
extensions, system of interventions and, 28

F

Five Dysfunctions of a Team, The (Lencioni), 27
Fundamentals: PBL module facilitator notes
    about, 61
    assessments, 63
    guiding questions, 64
    introduction to the event, 62
    learning objectives, 62
    problems, 62
    products, 62–63
    reproducibles for, 70–75
    resources, 64
    roles and responsibilities, 61–62
    time and schedules, 64–65

G

goals, 27, 57, 59–60
Goh, K., 3
grading, decision making within the school system, 101–103
growth mindset, 4
guaranteed and viable curriculum, 27–28
guiding questions
    elements of the PBL method and, 46
    Fundamentals: PBL module facilitator notes, 64
    Learning for All: PBL module facilitator notes, 107
    reproducibles for, 74–75, 95–97, 118–119
    Writing on the Wall: PBL module facilitator notes, 84

H

Hallinger, P., 42
Hattie, J., 25, 26
honoring and trusting team members, 20, 22–25, 36, 37
hope, 99
Hyatt, M., 58

I

integrating the learning of others, 20, 21, 32, 33
interventions, system of interventions and extensions, 28
introduction
    about positive thinking and action, 1
    about this book, 5
    alleviating decision fatigue, 3
    implementing a problem-based learning approach, 3–4
    making a difference, 4–5
    self-efficacy, 2
    shifting the thinking and PLCs at Work, 2–3
introduction to the event
    elements of the PBL method and, 43
    Fundamentals: PBL module facilitator notes, 62
    Learning for All: PBL module facilitator notes, 105
    Writing on the Wall: PBL module facilitator notes, 82

K

Kahneman, D., 100–101
Kanold, T., 20
knowing-doing gap, 16
Kohn, A., 20

L

Lambros, A., 41
leadership
    behaviors to build better job performance, 24
    loose and tight leadership, 25
learning. *See* shifting from teaching to learning
Learning for All: PBL module facilitator notes
    about, 104
    assessments, 106
    guiding questions, 107
    introduction to the event, 105
    learning objectives, 105
    problems, 105
    products, 105–106
    reproducibles for, 114–119
    resources, 107
    roles and responsibilities, 104–105
    time and schedules, 107–108
learning objectives
    elements of the PBL method and, 44
    Fundamentals: PBL module facilitator notes, 62, 63
    Learning for All: PBL module facilitator notes, 105, 106
    products and, 45
    Writing on the Wall: PBL module facilitator notes, 82, 83
Lencioni, P., 27
listening to learn, 20, 30, 31

M

Many, T., 2
Mattos, M., 2
McGonigal, K., 9
mission statements, 57, 58
Muhammad, A., 2

N

National Academies of Sciences, Engineering, and Medicine, 3
nonlearners, 10

P

PBL Learning Grid. *See also* problem-based learning (PBL)
    about, 48–50
    example learning grid for PLCs, 50–51
    reproducibles for, 70, 89, 114
PBL mindset. *See also* problem-based learning (PBL)
    about, xvi, 4
    change in thinking, 14–15
    elements of the PBL method and, 43
    honoring and trusting team members, 23
    listening to learn and, 20
    PBL Learning Grid, 48, 50
    professional development, 21
    reproducibles for, 53
    working collectively on specific items and, 80

PBL training modules. *See* shifting from intentions to results; shifting from isolation to collaboration; shifting from teaching to learning
perspective-taking, 20
PLC LIGHT
　　about, 19–20
　　growing professionally, 20, 21–22
　　honoring and trusting team members, 20, 22–25
　　integrating the learning of others, 20, 21
　　listening to learn, 20
PLC Lite, 19, 78
Popham, W., 28
Problem-Based Learning in K-8 Classrooms (Lambros), 41
problem-based learning (PBL). *See also* building a powerful partnership: PLC at Work and PBL; building collaborative skill power: problem-based learning; building collaborative willpower: learning to trust the PLC process using PBL
　　about, 12–14
　　characteristics of, 40–41
　　clarity and, xvi
　　collaborative teaming and, xvi–xvii
　　decision fatigue and, 3
　　elements of the PBL method, 43–48
　　implementing, 3–4
　　in K-12 education, 41–42
　　learning by doing and, xvi
　　PLC at Work and, xv
　　shifting the thinking in schools and, 2–3
problems
　　elements of the PBL method and, 43–44
　　Fundamentals: PBL module facilitator notes, 62
　　Learning for All: PBL module facilitator notes, 105
　　Writing on the Wall: PBL module facilitator notes, 82
products
　　elements of the PBL method and, 45–46
　　Fundamentals: PBL module facilitator notes, 62–63
　　Learning for All: PBL module facilitator notes, 105–106
　　Writing on the Wall: PBL module facilitator notes, 82–83
professional development, 20, 21–22, 34, 35
Professional Learning Communities at Work (PLCs at Work). *See also* building a powerful partnership: PLC at Work and PBL; building collaborative willpower: learning to trust the PLC process using PBL
　　about, 11
　　areas to monitor in, 26
　　big ideas of, 11–12, 99
　　clarity in, xvi
　　and collective teacher efficacy, 2
　　critical questions of, xvi–xvii, 12, 103
　　example learning grid for PLCs, 50–51
　　and the Fundamentals: PBL module facilitator notes, 61
　　and Learning for All: PBL module facilitator notes, 104
　　pillars of a PLC, 57–60
　　power of teaming in a PLC, xvi–xvii
　　and shifting the thinking in schools, 2–3
　　and student learning, xv
　　and working collectively on specific items, 79–80
　　and the Writing on the Wall: PBL module facilitator notes, 81
　　purpose of schools, xv, 57

R

reproducibles for
　　Fundamentals: scene 1, the, 71
　　Fundamentals: scene 2, the, 72
　　Fundamentals: scene 3, the, 73
　　guiding questions: Learning for All, 118–119
　　guiding questions: the Fundamentals, 74–75
　　guiding questions: the Writing on the Wall, 95–97
　　Learning for All: scene 1, 115
　　Learning for All: scene 2, 116
　　Learning for All: scene 3, 117
　　listening to learn tool, 30
　　PBL Learning Grid: Learning for All, 114
　　PBL Learning Grid: the Fundamentals, 70
　　PBL Learning Grid: the Writing on the Wall, 89
　　think this, do this: a systematic process, 86
　　think this, do this: collective commitments, 68
　　think this, do this: collectively interpret standards, 111
　　think this, do this: examining student proficiency, 112
　　think this, do this: focusing on student mastery, 113
　　think this, do this: goal setting, 69
　　think this, do this: growing professionally as individuals and as a team, 34
　　think this, do this: honoring and trusting your team members and the PLC process, 36
　　think this, do this: integrating the learning of others into your own understanding, 32
　　think this, do this: listening to learn, 31
　　think this, do this: PBL mindset, 53
　　think this, do this: practice, policy, and procedures, 67
　　think this, do this: the purpose of school, 66
　　think this, do this: turning intentions into actions, 109–110
　　think this, do this: working collectively on specific items, 88
　　think this, do this: working interdependently, 87
　　tool for growing professionally as individuals and as a team, 35
　　tool for honoring and trusting team members and the PLC process, 37
　　tool for integrating the learning of others with your own understanding, 33
　　Writing on the Wall: scene 1, the, 90–91
　　Writing on the Wall: scene 2, the, 92–93
　　Writing on the Wall: scene 3, the, 94
results, focus on, 12, 99, 103. *See also* shifting from intentions to results
resources
　　elements of the PBL method and, 45
　　Fundamentals: PBL module facilitator notes, 64
　　Learning for All: PBL module facilitator notes, 107
　　Writing on the Wall: PBL module facilitator notes, 84
roles and responsibilities
　　Fundamentals: PBL module facilitator notes, 61–62
　　Learning for All: PBL module facilitator notes, 104–105
　　Writing on the Wall: PBL module facilitator notes, 81–82

S

self-efficacy, 2, 25
Senge, P., 101, 102

shifting from intentions to results
    about, 99–100
    acting with intention: unit by unit, 103
    decisions making using data, 100–101
    decision making within the school system, 101–103
    learning for all, 103
    Learning for All: PBL module facilitator notes, 104–108
    reproducibles for, 109–119
    using data to inform, 101
shifting from isolation to collaboration. *See also* collaboration
    about, 77–78
    focus on collaboration, 80
    reproducibles for, 86–97
    systematic process of collaboration, 78
    working collectively on specific items, 79–80
    working interdependently, 78–79
    Writing on the Wall: PBL module facilitator notes, 81–85
shifting from teaching to learning
    about, 57
    focus on the fundamentals, 60
    four pillars of a PLC, 57–60
    Fundamentals: PBL module facilitator notes, 61–65
    reproducibles for, 66–75
SMART goals, 27, 59–60
standards
    determining essential standards, 103
    elements of the PBL method and, 45, 46
    reproducibles for, 111
system of interventions and extensions, 28

T

teaching. *See* shifting from teaching to learning
teams. *See* collaborative teams
Think This, Do This approach, 16
time and schedules
    elements of the PBL method and, 47–48
    Fundamentals: PBL module facilitator notes, 64–65
    Learning for All: PBL module facilitator notes, 107–108

    systematic process of collaboration and, 78
    Writing on the Wall: PBL module facilitator notes, 84–85
trust
    adult learners and, 10
    balance and trust, 15–16
    honoring and trusting team members, 20, 22–25, 36, 37
Trust Matters: Leadership for Successful Schools (Tschannen-Moran), 23
Tschannen-Moran, M., 23

V

values (collective commitments), 57, 59
vision, 57, 58–59
Vision-Driven Leader, The (Hyatt), 58

W

Wiliam, D., 28
willpower, definition of, 9. *See also* building collaborative willpower: learning to trust the PLC process using PBL
Willpower Instinct: How Self-Control Works, Why It Matters, and How to Get More of It, The (McGonigal), 9
Writing on the Wall: PBL module facilitator notes
    about, 81
    assessments, 83
    guiding questions, 84
    introduction to the event, 82
    learning objectives, 82
    problems, 82
    products, 82–83
    reproducibles for, 89–97
    resources, 84
    roles and responsibilities, 81–82
    time and schedules, 84–85

Y

Yew, E., 3

Z

Zak, P., 27

Learning by Doing
Richard DuFour, Rebecca DuFour, Robert Eaker, Thomas W. Many, Mike Mattos, and Anthony Muhammad

25 years on, the PLC at Work process continues to produce results across the United States and worldwide. In this fourth edition of the bestseller *Learning by Doing*, the authors use updated research and time-tested knowledge to address current education challenges, from learning gaps exacerbated by the COVID-19 pandemic to the need to drive a highly effective multitiered system of supports.

BKG169

Transforming School Culture
Anthony Muhammad

The second edition of this best-selling resource delivers powerful new insight into the four types of educators—Believers, Fundamentalists, Tweeners, and Survivors—and how to work with each group to create thriving schools. The book also includes Dr. Anthony Muhammad's latest research, as well as a new chapter dedicated to answering frequently asked questions on culture, leadership, and more.

BKF793

The Way Forward
Anthony Muhammad

Teachers today have a window of opportunity to shape education in a way that will impact the profession for generations. In this compelling and comprehensive book, educator and best-selling author Anthony Muhammad explores the educational hurdles of the past in the context of present-day concerns and envisions an education system where all schools energetically embrace the PLC at Work process.

BKG159

PLCs at Work and the IB Primary Years Programme
Edited by Timothy S. Stuart and David (Cal) Callaway

Dive into the possibilities of moving toward a personalized approach to education. With contributions from educators around the world, *PLCs at Work and the IB Primary Years Programme* examines practices from envelope-pushing schools within the International Baccalaureate Primary Years Programme and shows how the tenets of professional learning communities can ensure that all students learn at high levels.

BKG056

Simplifying the Journey
Bob Sonju, Maren Powers, and Sheline Miller

Smart educators know simplicity is key to mitigating overwhelm and ensuring success. This book will help. Access the proven PLC at Work process in a straightforward, easy-to-implement guide. Designated actions and essential steps for teachers, school leaders, and coaches focus on answering each of the four critical questions of a professional learning community so you can be confident you are doing the right work.

BKG118

Visit SolutionTree.com or call 800.733.6786 to order.

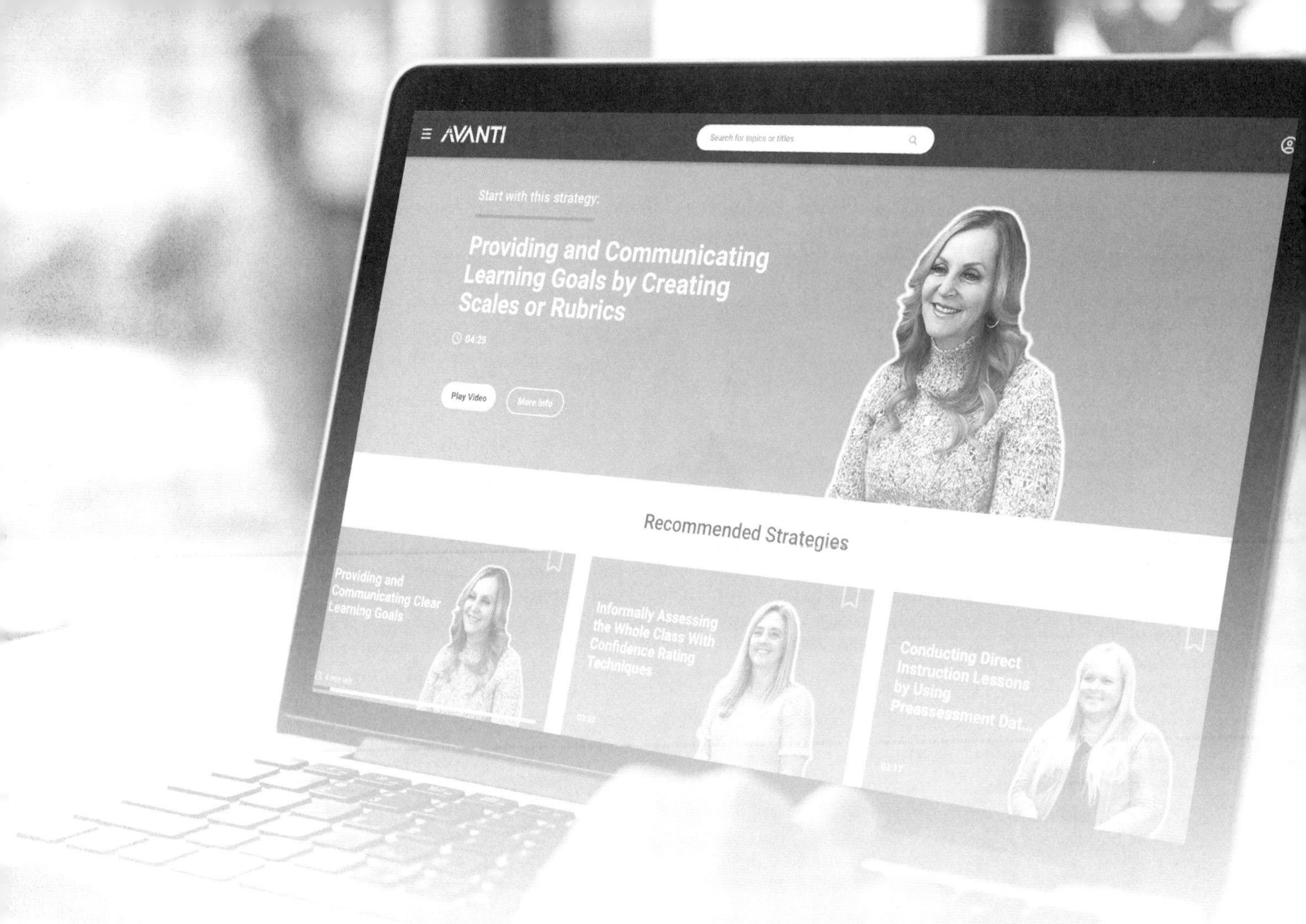

AVANTI

Grow your teacher toolkit by learning from other teachers

Take control of your professional growth and positively impact your students' lives with proven, ready-to-use classroom strategies. With Avanti, you'll get professional learning created by teachers, for teachers.

Learn more
My-Avanti.com/**GrowYourToolkit**